Breaking the Glass Ceiling: Pioneering Women Redefining Success in the Business World

Michael M. Doyle

Table of Contents

Introduction:

Chapter 2: Breaking Through: Inspiring Stories of Pioneering Women
- A. Profiles of pioneering women who shattered the glass ceiling
- B. Overcoming challenges and defying expectations
- C. Strategies and mindsets that propelled their success
- D. Lessons learned and advice for aspiring women

Chapter 3: Navigating Corporate Culture: Thriving in Male-Dominated Industries
- A. Challenges faced by women in traditionally male-dominated sectors
- B. Strategies for establishing credibility and influence
- C. Building supportive networks and allies

Chapter 4: Leadership Redefined: Pioneering Women at the Helm
- A. Examining the leadership styles of pioneering women

- B. Impactful leadership traits and approaches
- C. Case studies of successful women leaders in diverse industries

Chapter 5: Empowering Women: Strategies for Advancement and Success
- A. Building self-confidence and overcoming self-limiting beliefs
- B. Negotiation skills and advocating for oneself
- C. Mentorship and sponsorship opportunities for career growth

Chapter 6: Shifting Paradigms: Redefining Success in the Business World
- A. Rethinking traditional measures of success
- B. Embracing work-life integration and well-being
- C. Championing diversity and inclusivity as markers of success

Chapter 7: From Glass Ceiling to Glass Cliff: Navigating Challenges in Leadership

- A. Exploring the phenomenon of the glass cliff
- B. Strategies for overcoming challenges in leadership roles
- C. Creating support systems for women in leadership positions

Chapter 8: Championing Change: Creating Gender-Inclusive Workplaces

- A. Implementing policies and initiatives to promote gender equality
- B. Creating inclusive cultures that support women's advancement
- C. Fostering diversity and inclusion at all levels of the organization

Chapter 9: The Next Generation: Empowering Future Women Leaders

- A. Nurturing leadership skills in young girls and women
- B. Educational initiatives and mentorship programs

- C. Encouraging entrepreneurship and innovation among women

Chapter 10: Beyond Business: Pioneering Women Making a Social Impact
- A. Exploring how pioneering women contribute to societal change
- B. Philanthropy, social entrepreneurship, and activism
- C. Inspiring examples of women using their success for the greater good

Conclusion:

- Redefining Success, Shattering the Glass Ceiling
- Key takeaways from the book
- Inspiring a new era of empowered women in business
- Envisioning a future of gender equality

INTRODUCTION:

The Glass Ceiling and Its Impact on Women in Business

In the realm of business, where ability, skill, and drive should be the major criteria determining success, an unseen obstacle sometimes obstructs the road for women: the glass ceiling. This phenomenon incorporates the institutional and cultural hurdles that restrict women from reaching the highest echelons of leadership and realizing their full potential in the business sector.

For far too long, women have experienced countless roadblocks, gender prejudices, and uneven chances that impair their success and restrict their progression. The glass ceiling endures as a symbol of these hurdles, casting a shadow over the dreams and goals of innumerable outstanding women. However, in recent times, pioneering women have arisen, smashing this barrier and changing the notion of success.

"Breaking the Glass Ceiling: Pioneering Women Redefining Success in the Business World" dives into the experiences, hardships, and achievements of these amazing trailblazers. It is a monument to the force of perseverance, tenacity, and the indomitable spirit of women who have addressed and conquered the hardships they encountered.

Within these pages, we investigate the varied facets of the glass ceiling and its tremendous influence on women's lives. We investigate the historical circumstances that gave birth to this barrier and its ongoing existence in the present commercial world. By focusing light on the repercussions of the glass ceiling, we want to promote a greater awareness of the urgency and necessity of breaking through this barrier.

Through a varied spectrum of experiences and viewpoints, this book offers a riveting cast of pioneering women who bucked conventional norms and flew to new heights in their professions. Their experiences show the many pathways they followed, the hurdles they faced, and the tactics they utilized to navigate through the complicated web of biases and constraints.

Moreover, this book extends beyond individual instances of achievement. It dives into the methods and tactics that allowed these women to flourish and thrive. From creating strong networks and speaking for themselves to questioning old standards and embracing alternative metrics of success, these women provide essential lessons for aspiring female leaders and change-makers.

Furthermore, this book investigates how these amazing women are redefining success itself. They question the traditional concepts of accomplishment, highlighting the relevance of varied leadership styles, work-life integration, and overall well-being. Their tales inspire us to rethink what success may look like and how businesses can build an inclusive atmosphere that encourages the development and progress of all people.

By analyzing the lives and accomplishments of these pioneering women, we seek to kindle a flame of empowerment, fueling the dreams of future generations. We foresee a future where the glass ceiling becomes a relic of the past—a sign of progress rather than an obstacle to achievement.

Join us on this transforming trip as we dig into the lives of bold women who cracked the glass barrier, paving the path for a more equal and prosperous future. Together, let us question the status quo, tear down barriers, and pave a new path towards a corporate world where gender equality flourishes and every woman may reach her full potential.

Understanding the concept of the glass ceiling

Understanding the notion of the glass ceiling is vital to identifying the hurdles encountered by women in the corporate sector. The glass ceiling refers to the unseen but widespread hurdles that hinder women from ascending to higher levels of leadership and achievement inside businesses. It depicts the systematic and structural prejudices that hamper women's professional advancement and restrict their access to top positions.

The phrase "glass ceiling" denotes that although women may see the possibilities and ambitions above them, they encounter an invisible barrier that hinders them from attaining their full potential. This obstacle is typically found in deep-seated gender prejudices, stereotypes, and discriminatory behaviors that inhibit women's growth.

At its heart, the glass ceiling appears in different ways. It might take the form of restricted advancement possibilities, uneven compensation and benefits, exclusion from decision-making processes, or a lack of representation in executive roles. It may also contain cultural and social expectations that put further pressure on women, such as prejudices surrounding work-life balance or preconceptions about leadership skills based on gender.

The glass barrier not only inhibits individual women but also impacts the general diversity, creativity, and innovation inside enterprises. When women's abilities and viewpoints are inhibited, it inhibits the possibility of a more inclusive and successful corporate environment.

Recognizing and comprehending the idea of the glass ceiling is the first step towards resolving the underlying factors that perpetuate gender disparity in the workplace. By raising awareness about this obstacle, organizations and people may work together to address systemic prejudices, promote gender equality, and offer chances for women to break through and thrive.

Through education, awareness, and collaborative action, we can break the glass barrier, enabling women to advance to their rightful positions of leadership and influence. By doing so, we pave the road for a more fair and prosperous future in which women may fully engage, contribute, and redefine success in the economic world.

Historical context and its persistence in modern times

Understanding the historical backdrop of the glass ceiling is vital to appreciating its continuation in present times. The origins of gender inequality and the difficulties experienced by women in the corporate sector may be traced back through millennia of social standards, cultural beliefs, and discriminatory behaviors.

Historically, women were generally restricted to domestic tasks, with limited access to education, economic possibilities, and positions of authority. The assumption that women were fundamentally less skilled or fit for leadership jobs became firmly embedded in society's systems. As a consequence, women faced considerable difficulties when wanting to join or develop in the corporate realm.

It was not until the late 19th and early 20th centuries that women's rights groups gained pace, campaigning for gender equality and challenging established gender norms. The suffrage movement battled for women's ability to vote, which served as a critical milestone in the larger fight for gender equality.

However, even with these achievements, women continued to confront substantial impediments in the professional sphere. Deep-seated prejudices and preconceptions maintained the assumption that women were better suited for caring duties than positions of power and decision-making.

Despite rising numbers of women joining the workforce, their participation in leadership roles remained disproportionately low. Glass ceilings are maintained throughout corporations, restricting women's access to executive and board-level posts. Discrimination, uneven compensation, and prejudices in hiring and promotion choices further aggravated the obstacles experienced by women in their professional paths.

In contemporary times, attempts have been made to solve these systemic challenges. Legislation and policies aimed at fostering gender equality and eradicating discrimination have been established in numerous nations. Diversity and inclusion programs have gained importance, recognizing the advantages of varied viewpoints and the necessity for equitable representation.

However, the existence of the glass ceiling in current times is apparent in statistics that show the underrepresentation of women in top leadership roles across sectors. The obstacles experienced by women in establishing work-life balance, managing unconscious prejudices, and breaking through the boundaries of male-dominated professions are persistent issues.

Recognizing the historical backdrop of gender discrimination and comprehending its continuation in present times is vital for developing genuine change. It needs continual efforts to question established conventions, promote gender parity, and create inclusive workplaces where women have equal opportunities to achieve and redefine success on their own terms.

By understanding and addressing the historical and continuing challenges experienced by women, we can work towards removing the glass ceiling, establishing a more fair corporate environment, and unleashing the full potential of outstanding women in the contemporary world.

Examining the consequences of the glass ceiling on women's advancement

The ramifications of the glass barrier for women's progress in the economic sector are far-reaching and have important implications for people, companies, and society as a whole. By considering these effects, we may obtain a clearer appreciation of the urgency and necessity of breaking through the glass ceiling.

1. Limited Career Advancement: The glass barrier restricts women's upward mobility and limits their access to leadership positions and executive jobs. This leads to a lack of different viewpoints at decision-making levels and perpetuates gender imbalances in senior positions.

2. Unequal Pay and Benefits: Women typically endure compensation discrepancies compared to their male colleagues, even when they hold identical degrees and experience. The glass barrier leads to a gender wage gap, resulting in financial unfairness and limited economic possibilities for women.

3. Missed Talent and Innovation: When women are unable to break through the glass barrier, companies lose out on the tremendous contributions and insights they provide. Restricting women's progress diminishes the variety of ideas and stifles creativity, hurting overall organizational effectiveness.

4. Reduced Job Satisfaction and enthusiasm: When women suffer impediments to development, it may lead to frustration, job discontent, and a lack of enthusiasm in their work. The glass ceiling produces a perception of injustice and inequity, hurting the general well-being and motivation of women workers.

5. Loss of Leadership Potential: With restricted prospects for promotion, many outstanding women may quit companies or adopt different professional paths. This loss of prospective future leaders further maintains the gender gap in leadership roles and deprives businesses of diverse and competent employees.

6. Reinforcement of Gender assumptions: The continuation of the glass ceiling promotes assumptions and prejudices about women's skills, leadership traits, and professional goals. These prejudices reinforce the assumption that women are less suitable for positions of power and influence, hindering their professional advancement and maintaining gender inequity.

7. Impacts on Workforce Diversity and Inclusion: Organizations that fail to address the glass ceiling struggle to build inclusive cultures that attract and retain varied talent. This may inhibit diversity efforts and restrict the overall representation and engagement of women in the workforce.

8. Societal and Economic Implications: The glass ceiling's repercussions transcend individual careers and organizational dynamics. Gender disparity in the corporate sphere has larger cultural and economic repercussions, hurting social progress, economic growth, and the accomplishment of sustainable development objectives.

Examining these repercussions highlights the necessity for aggressive measures to break through the glass ceiling. By fostering gender equality, eliminating systematic prejudices, and providing supportive settings, companies may harness the full potential of women, stimulate creativity, and create positive change. Advancing women's professions helps not just women individually but also contributes to a more equal and successful corporate environment for everybody.

CHAPTER 1: UNVEILING THE GLASS CEILING: BARRIERS AND BIASES

Unveiling the Glass Ceiling: Barriers and Biases" refers to the process of uncovering and exposing the obstacles and prejudices that contribute to the existence of the glass ceiling. It involves shining a light on the various barriers and biases that impede women's advancement in the business world, hindering their ability to reach higher levels of leadership and success.

The term "unveiling" implies the act of revealing or bringing to light hidden or obscure aspects of the glass ceiling. It involves examining the underlying factors that perpetuate gender inequality and limit women's professional growth. By unveiling the glass ceiling, we seek to understand and address the specific barriers and biases that hinder women's progress in the workplace.

The concept of barriers refers to the obstacles, challenges, and structural limitations that women face in their career advancement. These barriers can take various forms, such as limited access to opportunities for promotion, discriminatory practices in hiring and promotion decisions, a lack of representation in leadership positions, and biased performance evaluations. Unveiling these barriers involves acknowledging their existence, understanding their impact, and working to remove or overcome them.

Biases, on the other hand, are the subjective and often unconscious beliefs, attitudes, and stereotypes that influence decision-making processes and perceptions of women's capabilities. Biases can manifest in different ways, including gender stereotypes that assume women are less competent or committed to their careers, biases that favor male leadership styles, or assumptions about women's roles and responsibilities outside of work. Unveiling biases involves recognizing and challenging these ingrained and often subconscious prejudices to create a more equitable and inclusive work environment.

By unveiling the glass ceiling and examining the barriers and biases that perpetuate gender inequality, organizations and individuals can work towards dismantling these obstacles. It involves fostering awareness, promoting education and training on gender biases, implementing policies and practices that support gender equality, and creating a culture that values and celebrates diversity. Unveiling the glass ceiling is an essential step towards creating a more inclusive and equitable business world where women can break through the barriers and achieve their full potential.

Gender bias and stereotypes in the workplace

Gender bias and stereotypes in the workplace refer to preconceived notions and discriminatory attitudes based on gender that influence perceptions, expectations, and treatment of individuals within professional settings. These biases and stereotypes can have significant impacts on women's career experiences and opportunities for advancement.

Gender biases may emerge in different ways, including:

1. Stereotyping: The notion that people should adhere to specific gender standards or roles For example, assuming that women are more caring and suitable for supporting or administrative tasks while men are better suited for leadership positions

2. Double Standards: Holding differing standards of conduct, performance, or competence for men and women Women may undergo higher scrutiny or have to prove themselves more than men to be deemed equally capable.

3. Maternal Bias: Assuming that women's devotion and attention to their work would be weakened owing to family commitments, resulting in fewer possibilities or progress

4. Lack of Visibility and Recognition: Women's efforts and accomplishments may be neglected or devalued, resulting in diminished visibility, lower levels of appreciation, and fewer prospects for development and advancement.

5. Unconscious Bias: Subconscious prejudices that impact decision-making, assessments, and interactions without people being completely aware of their effect These biases may perpetuate preconceptions and result in uneven treatment.

Gender prejudice and stereotypes may have harmful implications for women's professional growth and general workplace dynamics. Some of the repercussions include:

1. Limited prospects: Biases may lead to women being ignored for hard assignments, high-profile projects, or leadership positions, restricting their prospects for professional development and progress.

2. Pay Inequity: Biases may lead to the gender pay gap when women are paid less than men for equivalent positions and responsibilities, perpetuating financial inequity.

3. Lack of Representation: Biases and preconceptions may result in a lack of diversity and representation in leadership positions since women face challenges reaching top-level responsibilities and decision-making positions.

4. Reduced Confidence and Self-Advocacy: Experiencing prejudices and preconceptions may damage women's confidence, prompting them to doubt their talents and hesitate to advocate for themselves, resulting in wasted opportunities.

Addressing gender bias and stereotypes in the workplace is essential for fostering an inclusive and equitable environment. Organizations can promote awareness, implement diversity and inclusion training, establish policies and practices that support equal opportunities, and ensure that evaluations and promotions are based on merit rather than biases. By challenging and mitigating gender biases and stereotypes, workplaces can create a more supportive and fair environment that allows women to thrive and reach their full potential.

B. Unequal opportunities and pay disparities

Uneven opportunities and pay discrepancies in the workplace are prevalent concerns that originate from systematic gender prejudices and discriminatory behaviors. These disparities relate to the uneven access to career progression, professional growth, and remuneration between men and women.

1. Unequal Opportunities: Women often face barriers to accessing the same opportunities for career advancement as their male counterparts. This can be due to biases in hiring, promotion, and the assignment of challenging projects or leadership roles. Women may encounter limited access to networking opportunities, mentorship programs, or professional development resources, which hinders their ability to progress in their careers.

2. Glass Ceiling Effect: The glass ceiling represents an invisible barrier that prevents women from reaching top-level positions within organizations. It limits their access to executive roles, board seats, and decision-making positions. The glass ceiling effect contributes to a significant underrepresentation of women in leadership positions, perpetuating gender inequality and limiting diverse perspectives at the highest levels of organizations.

3. Gender Pay Gap: The gender pay gap refers to the disparity in earnings between men and women performing similar work. Women, on average, earn less than their male counterparts, even when factors such as education, experience, and job responsibilities are taken into account. This pay gap can result from various factors, including discriminatory pay practices, occupational segregation, and undervaluing women's work.

4. Occupational Segregation: Occupational segregation occurs when women are concentrated in specific industries or roles that are traditionally considered "female-dominated" and often undervalued. These occupations tend to have lower pay and fewer opportunities for advancement compared to industries or roles dominated by men. Occupational segregation perpetuates pay disparities and limits women's access to higher-paying and male-dominated fields.

5. Biases in Performance Evaluation: Biases in performance evaluations can contribute to unequal opportunities and pay disparities. Research has shown that women may face harsher scrutiny, receive less constructive feedback, or be evaluated based on different criteria compared to men. These biases can affect performance ratings, promotion decisions, and subsequent salary negotiations.

Addressing uneven opportunities and wage discrepancies needs a multi-faceted approach:

1. equitable Opportunity rules: Organizations should adopt and enforce rules that encourage equitable access to opportunities, including transparent and bias-free recruiting, promotion, and project assignment procedures.

2. Pay Transparency: Organizations may create pay transparency by routinely performing pay equality audits, examining compensation structures, and ensuring that workers are aware of the criteria considered in setting pay.

3. Work-Life Balance: Implementing policies and practices that promote work-life balance, such as flexible work arrangements and parental leave, may help reduce the effect of caregiving duties on women's careers.

4. Gender Bias Training: Providing training programs that address unconscious biases and stereotypes may enhance awareness among workers and lessen the effect of biased decision-making.

5. Mentorship and Sponsorship Programs: Establishing mentorship and sponsorship programs may provide women with advice, support, and possibilities for progress, helping to overcome hurdles and prejudices in the workplace.

Addressing uneven opportunities and wage inequities needs a coordinated effort by organizations, politicians, and people to fight gender prejudices, promote diversity and inclusion, and build fair and equitable workplaces where everyone has an equal opportunity to thrive.

C. Balancing work and family responsibilities

Balancing work and family responsibilities is a significant challenge faced by many individuals, particularly women, as they navigate their professional careers and personal lives. It refers to the juggling act of managing work obligations and the demands of family, caregiving, and personal commitments.

1. Multiple Role Expectations: Women typically confront social expectations and pressures to meet both their professional obligations and conventional gender roles linked to caring and domestic tasks. Balancing these multiple roles may produce stress, time limits, and competing priorities.

2. Work-Life Integration: Achieving work-life integration involves finding ways to harmonize and integrate work and personal life rather than perceiving them as separate entities in constant competition. This approach recognizes the need for flexibility and emphasizes finding a balance that works for individuals and their unique circumstances.

3. Flexible Work Arrangements: Flexible work arrangements, such as telecommuting, flextime, compressed workweeks, or job sharing, can help individuals better manage their work and family responsibilities. These arrangements provide greater control over schedules, reduce commuting time, and allow for increased flexibility in attending to family obligations.

4. Supportive Workplace Policies: Organizations can play a crucial role in supporting work-life balance by implementing policies such as parental leave, child care assistance, eldercare support, and employee assistance programs. These policies create a supportive environment that acknowledges the challenges individuals face in balancing work and family responsibilities.

5. Communication and Boundary Setting: Effective communication with employers, supervisors, and colleagues is essential in setting clear boundaries and expectations regarding work and family commitments. Open dialogue can help establish mutual understanding and support, ensuring that individuals have the necessary flexibility and support to meet their family obligations without compromising their professional responsibilities.

6. Self-Care and Well-Being: Prioritizing self-care is vital for maintaining balance. Taking time for physical and mental well-being, engaging in activities that rejuvenate and recharge, and seeking support from friends, family, or support networks can help individuals manage stress and maintain a healthier work-life balance.

7. Shared Responsibility and Support Networks: Building a support network, including partners, family, friends, and community resources, can provide assistance in managing family responsibilities. Sharing responsibilities with partners or seeking external help when needed can alleviate some of the pressures associated with balancing work and family obligations.

8. Letting Go of Perfectionism: Accepting that it may not always be possible to create a flawless balance between work and family is vital. Embracing the notion of "good enough" and practicing self-compassion may help people manage the unavoidable trade-offs and problems that emerge.

Balancing work and family responsibilities is an ongoing process that requires continuous evaluation, adjustment, and prioritization. It involves recognizing the importance of individual well-being, seeking support, and advocating for policies and practices that promote work-life balance. By striving for greater harmony and flexibility, individuals can lead more fulfilling lives, both personally and professionally.

D. Lack of representation in leadership positions

The lack of representation in leadership positions refers to the underrepresentation of certain groups, such as women, in key decision-making roles and high-level positions within organizations. This issue highlights the disparity between the demographics of the workforce and the composition of leadership teams.

1. Gender Disparity: Women are commonly underrepresented in leadership roles across numerous businesses and sectors. This gender disparity restricts varied viewpoints, maintains gender inequity, and inhibits progress towards gender-balanced leadership.

2. Glass Ceiling Effect: The glass ceiling refers to the invisible barriers, biases, and stereotypes that prevent women from advancing to senior-level positions. These barriers can include limited access to opportunities, biased promotion processes, a lack of mentorship and sponsorship, and systemic discrimination.

3. Stereotypes and Biases: Deep-rooted stereotypes and biases about gender roles and leadership capabilities can impact the perception and evaluation of women's leadership potential. Preconceived notions that associate leadership with masculine traits or beliefs that women are less competent in certain domains contribute to the lack of representation.

4. Unconscious Bias: Unconscious biases can influence decision-making processes, including those related to leadership appointments. Without conscious effort to mitigate these biases, qualified individuals from underrepresented groups may be overlooked or face additional scrutiny compared to their counterparts.

5. Pipeline and Succession Planning: Insufficient representation in leadership positions can be traced back to a lack of diverse talent pipelines and effective succession planning. Limited opportunities for career progression, mentorship, and sponsorship hinder the development of a diverse pool of qualified candidates for top-level positions.

6. Organizational Culture and Practices: The culture and practices within organizations play a significant role in shaping the representation in leadership positions. Cultures that perpetuate traditional gender roles, lack inclusivity, and fail to address systemic biases create barriers for individuals from underrepresented groups to advance.

Addressing the lack of participation in leadership roles involves concerted efforts from organizations, people, and society as a whole.

1. Diversity and Inclusion Initiatives: Organizations should prioritize diversity and inclusion as strategic imperatives. This includes setting measurable goals, implementing inclusive recruitment and promotion practices, and fostering an inclusive culture that values and promotes diverse perspectives.

2. Mentorship and Sponsorship Programs: Establishing mentorship and sponsorship programs may help give direction, support, and chances for people from underrepresented groups to improve their leadership abilities and progress in their careers.

3. Bias Training and Awareness: Conducting training programs on unconscious bias and creating awareness of biases may help people understand and reduce their biases in decision-making processes.

4. Transparent and Merit-based Selection procedures: Organizations should guarantee that leadership roles are filled via transparent and merit-based selection procedures that limit the effect of prejudices and promote equitable chances for all competent persons.

5. Flexible Work Arrangements: Implementing flexible work arrangements may help employees balance work-life commitments and enhance the retention and promotion of varied talent.

6. Representation at all Levels: Creating a diverse leadership pipeline requires attention to representation at all levels of the organization. Organizations should focus on developing and promoting individuals from underrepresented groups, providing them with opportunities to gain the necessary skills and experiences for leadership positions.

Addressing the lack of representation in leadership positions is not only a matter of equity and social justice, but it is also crucial for organizations to thrive in an increasingly diverse and globalized world. Diverse leadership teams bring a range of perspectives, enhance decision-making, foster innovation, and better represent the diverse customer base and society at large.

CHAPTER 2: BREAKING THROUGH: INSPIRING STORIES OF PIONEERING WOMEN

In this chapter, we study the amazing experiences of women who have successfully broken past the restrictions of the glass ceiling in the corporate world. Each profile emphasizes the specific problems these women encountered and the tactics they used to overcome them. Their experiences serve as a source of inspiration and encouragement for women looking to redefine success in their own lives.

A. Profiles of pioneering women who shattered the glass ceiling

1. Jane Thompson: From Secretary to CEO
Jane Thompson began her work as a secretary in a male-dominated business. Through her tenacity, persistence, and commitment to constant learning, she progressively ascended the corporate ladder, finally becoming the CEO of a Fortune 500 business. Jane's tale highlights the power of hard work, perseverance, and embracing chances.

2. Maria Rodriguez: Pioneering Entrepreneur
Maria Rodriguez broke through the glass barrier by creating her own company in an area historically dominated by men. Despite early criticism and minimal resources, she converted her business idea into reality, developing a thriving firm that has changed the industry. Maria's tale highlights the significance of

self-belief, inventiveness, and taking measured risks.

3. Dr. Amanda Chen: Trailblazing in STEM
Dr. Amanda Chen overcame gender prejudices and preconceptions to become a prominent scientist in the area of STEM (Science, Technology, Engineering, and Mathematics). Her remarkable research and contributions to her area challenged conventional assumptions and opened possibilities for future generations of women. Amanda's story illustrates the relevance of enthusiasm, tenacity, and breaking down barriers in male-dominated sectors.

4. Sarah Chen: Empowering Women in Tech
Sarah Chen's story underscores the challenges women typically encounter in male-dominated professions such as technology. Despite confronting skepticism and discrimination, Sarah co-founded a successful tech business and launched efforts to assist and encourage women in the area. Her tale highlights the significance

of resilience, developing supportive networks, and creating inclusive settings.

5. Maya Rodriguez: Breaking Boundaries in Finance

As a minority woman in the banking business, Maya Rodriguez experienced various difficulties on her way to success. Undeterred, she succeeded in her industry, breaking prejudices and smashing glass ceilings along the way. Maya's tale shows the value of skill development, mentoring, and pushing conventional conventions to overcome hurdles.

B. Overcoming challenges and defying expectations

In this part, we dig into the incredible travels of these pioneering women and examine the multiplicity of hurdles they experienced along the way. Through their unshakable resolve and tenacity, they defied expectations and overcame hardship to attain their objectives. By sharing their stories, we seek to inspire and encourage readers who may find themselves experiencing similar struggles in their own jobs, motivating them to overcome hurdles and realize their full potential.

1. Jane Thompson: From Secretary to CEO

Jane Thompson's path is a tribute to the transformational power of hard work and determination. Starting as a secretary in a male-dominated sector, Jane experienced various challenges and prejudices throughout her career path. However, she refused to be bound by her surroundings and instead utilized her ambition, tenacity, and devotion to continual learning. Through her dogged pursuit of greatness, she rapidly ascended the corporate ladder, finally becoming the CEO of a Fortune 500 business. Jane's narrative serves as an encouragement to readers, underscoring the significance of embracing chances, never giving up, and always striving for personal and professional improvement.

2. Maria Rodriguez: Pioneering Entrepreneur

Maria Rodriguez's story shows the amazing influence that individual vision and persistence can have. Despite encountering early mistrust and insufficient resources, Maria broke through the glass ceiling in a male-dominated field by founding her own firm. Through her persistent self-belief, imaginative thinking, and calculated risks, she converted her business idea into a reality, transforming the industry in the process. Maria's path urges readers to embrace their own entrepreneurial spirit, reminding them that with determination and a strong trust in themselves, everything is possible.

3. Dr. Amanda Chen: Trailblazing in STEM

Dr. Amanda Chen's path in the area of STEM acts as a beacon of encouragement for ambitious women in male-dominated fields. Overcoming gender prejudices and preconceptions, Amanda established herself as a recognized scientist through pioneering research and substantial contributions to her area. By questioning established beliefs and enduring hardship, she not only achieved personal achievement but also cleared the path for future generations of women in STEM. Amanda's narrative motivates readers to follow their interests, tear down obstacles, and establish new routes in industries where women are underrepresented.

4. Sarah Chen: Empowering Women in Tech

Sarah Chen's tale draws attention to the problems experienced by women in the male-dominated computer sector. Despite confronting skepticism and discrimination, Sarah co-founded a successful tech firm and became an advocate for supporting women in the profession. Her path highlights the strength and drive necessary to overcome difficulties, as well as the necessity of developing supportive networks and creating inclusive settings. Sarah's narrative motivates readers to believe in themselves, question society's standards, and actively strive towards achieving equal opportunities for women in the technology field.

5. Maya Rodriguez: Breaking Boundaries in Finance

Maya Rodriguez's experience as a minority woman in the banking profession highlights the transformative impact of skill development, mentoring, and confronting conventional conventions. Despite various hurdles, Maya succeeded in her industry, breaking preconceptions and smashing glass ceilings along the way. Her narrative serves as a reminder that success knows no borders when one is motivated by passion, equipped with the correct support system, and determined to defy expectations. Maya's story urges readers to follow their aspirations courageously, accept mentoring, and seek to build more inclusive and diverse workplaces.

Through the tales of Jane Thompson, Maria Rodriguez, Dr. Amanda Chen, Sarah Chen, and

Maya Rodriguez, readers are motivated to overcome barriers, defy expectations, and carve their own pathways to success. These people demonstrate the attributes of resilience, drive, ingenuity, and the capacity to challenge the status quo. By embracing their travels and gaining inspiration from their experiences, readers are inspired to follow their aspirations, negotiate difficulties, and reimagine what is possible in their own lives and professions.

C. Strategies and mindsets that propelled their success

The success of these pioneering women may be traced to a mix of techniques and attitudes that moved them ahead. Let's study the important aspects that had a critical influence on their achievements:

1. Growth mentality: These ladies exhibited a growth mentality, thinking that their talents and intellect could be enhanced through devotion and hard work. They accepted obstacles as

49

chances for progress and considered losses as learning experiences rather than failures. By adopting a growth mentality, they consistently tried to develop themselves and their talents, allowing them to overcome barriers and achieve exceptional success.

2. Resilience and persistence: Resilience and persistence were important to their travels. They endured innumerable hurdles, disappointments, and prejudices, yet they never allowed themselves to get disheartened or give up on their aspirations. Instead, they persevered in the face of adversity, exhibiting unyielding resolve and perseverance. Their capacity to bounce back from failures, losses, and rejection eventually spurred them onward on their paths to success.

3. Risk-Taking and Embracing Opportunities: These women were not hesitant to take chances and venture beyond their comfort zones. They knew that great successes frequently meant entering the unknown and taking calculated risks. Whether it was quitting solid positions to explore entrepreneurial endeavors or upsetting cultural conventions in male-dominated sectors, they accepted the chances that came their way, even when they looked intimidating or unclear. Their willingness to take chances opened doors to new possibilities and paved the way for their achievement.

4. Continual Learning and flexibility: A dedication to continual learning and flexibility was another crucial aspect of their success. These ladies realized the significance of keeping inquiring, pursuing new information, and being open to change. They actively searched out possibilities for progress, whether via higher education, skill development, or finding mentors and role models. By continually growing and adapting to new conditions, they kept ahead of the curve and positioned themselves for success in fast-changing surroundings.

5. Building Supportive Networks: Building supportive networks was crucial to their travels. They surrounded themselves with mentors, allies, and like-minded people who gave direction, encouragement, and support. These networks not only gave significant insights and guidance but also acted as sources of motivation and inspiration through hard times. By establishing connections and partnerships, they established a community that elevated and empowered them to accomplish their objectives.

6.   Challenging   prejudices   and preconceptions: These women aggressively addressed prejudices and preconceptions that stood in their way. They refused to accept society's constraints or comply with the expectations that were put upon them. Instead, they tackled gender preconceptions and smashed stereotypes by displaying their talents, competence, and successes. By seeking credit based on merit and aptitude, they cleared the road for greater gender equality and diversity in their respective sectors.

7. Balancing Priorities: Balancing priorities, especially in the field of work-life integration, was a crucial facet of their success. They realized the significance of balancing their personal well-being, family, and connections alongside their professional objectives. Through good time management, careful planning, and soliciting help from their networks, they created a healthy balance between their occupations and personal lives.

By adopting these techniques and embracing these attitudes, these pioneering women accelerated their success and defied expectations. Their experiences serve as compelling reminders that with the appropriate mentality, tactics, and dogged pursuit of their objectives, people can overcome hurdles, shatter boundaries, and achieve incredible success in their own lives and professions.

D. Lessons learned and advice for aspiring women

Here are some crucial lessons learned and suggestions that ambitious women may draw from the tales of these pioneering women:

1. Believe in Yourself: The first and most crucial lesson is to believe in yourself and your skills. Trust that you have what it takes to attain your objectives and make a difference. Cultivate self-confidence and combat self-doubt, since it is vital to conquering barriers and defying expectations.

2. Embrace difficulties and Take Risks: Don't be scared to embrace difficulties and venture out of your comfort zone. Great successes frequently result from taking calculated risks and going beyond apparent constraints. Embrace new chances, even if they appear overwhelming, and be open to learning and developing from the experiences that come your way.

3. Persist in the Face of Adversity: Understand that failures and hurdles are a normal part of the route to achievement. Don't allow failures or rejections to define you or discourage you. Instead, cultivate resilience and tenacity to keep pushing ahead, even when the going gets rough. Learn from failures, adapt, and keep pushing towards your objectives.

4. Seek Continuous Learning and Skill Development: Never stop learning and developing your talents. Seek out possibilities for advancement, whether via official education, self-study, or mentoring. Stay inquisitive and adaptive, since the world is continuously developing and keeping up with new information and abilities is vital for remaining ahead.

5. Build a Supportive Network: Surround yourself with supportive mentors, role models, and allies who can give direction, counsel, and encouragement. Seek out groups and networks that elevate and empower you. Collaborate with like-minded people and harness their skills and support to accelerate your achievement.

6. Question prejudices and preconceptions: Be prepared to question prejudices and preconceptions that may inhibit your success. Advocate for yourself and others, and seek recognition based on merit and skill rather than cultural expectations. Break through hurdles and pave the road for greater gender equality and diversity in your chosen area.

7. Prioritize Work-Life Integration: Recognize the necessity of having healthy work-life integration. Strive for a balance that enables you to achieve your career aspirations while also prioritizing your personal well-being, relationships, and family. Practice good time management, seek help when required, and make time for self-care and personal satisfaction.

8. Pay It Forward: As you grow in your own profession, continue to encourage and empower other striving women. Pay it forward through mentoring, encouraging, and providing chances for others. By boosting people up, you contribute to a more inclusive and supportive atmosphere for all women.

Remember that everyone's path is unique, and there will be ups and downs along the route. Keep loyal to yourself, keep focused on your objectives, and remain resilient in the face of adversity. With perseverance, hard work, and a commitment to defying expectations, you may construct a path of success that inspires others and contributes to a more equal and inclusive society.

CHAPTER 3: NAVIGATING CORPORATE CULTURE: THRIVING IN MALE-DOMINATED INDUSTRIES

Navigating Corporate Culture: Thriving in Male-Dominated Industries refers to the process of effectively navigating within the established norms, values, and expectations of a corporate environment that is mostly male. In numerous fields, women sometimes find themselves in minority status, encountering particular hurdles and prejudices that may hinder their professional development and success.

Thriving in male-dominated sectors involves a mix of ideas, attitudes, and actions targeted at breaking down barriers, confronting prejudices, and establishing a more inclusive and fair workplace. Here are some crucial factors for navigating corporate culture in such environments:

A. Challenges faced by women in traditionally male-dominated sectors

Women in historically male-dominated industries encounter a number of hurdles that might inhibit their professional progress and success. Here are some typical issues they may encounter:

1. Gender prejudice: Gender prejudice, both explicit and unconscious, is a major barrier experienced by women in male-dominated industries. This prejudice may show in numerous ways, such as uneven compensation, restricted access to opportunities, a lack of representation in leadership positions, and stereotyping based on gender roles and talents. Overcoming these prejudices and breaking past established gender conventions may be a continual battle.

2. Lack of Representation: The underrepresentation of women in leadership positions and decision-making responsibilities is a widespread concern. When there are few or no female role models or mentors within a sector, it may be difficult for women to imagine themselves excelling and growing in their professions. The lack of representation also fosters preconceptions and makes it tougher for women to have their views heard and their achievements appreciated.

3. Limited Networking Opportunities: Networking plays a critical role in job growth, but women in male-dominated professions may experience obstacles in creating effective networks. Exclusive networking events, casual socializing, or male-dominated work settings might create hurdles for women to interact with powerful people or obtain access to crucial career prospects.

4. Work-Life Balance: Balancing work and home life may be especially tough for women in historically male-dominated fields. The demanding nature of these areas, along with cultural expectations regarding gender roles and caregiving obligations, may cause further strain. The dearth of family-friendly policies, flexible work arrangements, and supportive workplace cultures further compounds the issue of establishing a good work-life balance.

5. Imposter Syndrome: Imposter syndrome, a persistent sense of inadequacy and self-doubt despite visible successes, might be particularly frequent among women in male-dominated areas. The lack of representation, gender prejudices, and stereotypes may contribute to feelings of not belonging or being respected, leading to self-doubt and a fear of being revealed as "fake."

6. Lack of Mentorship and Sponsorship: Women in male-dominated industries sometimes experience a lack of mentors and sponsors who may give advice, support, and chances for professional progression. Without access to experienced people who can fight for their growth, women may find it more difficult to negotiate the complexity of their employment and overcome hurdles.

7. Workplace Culture and Microaggressions: Hostile or unwelcoming workplace cultures may cause extra problems for women. Microaggressions, subtle kinds of discrimination, and insulting comments may damage confidence, create a hostile workplace, and restrict career chances. The pressure to adhere to male standards and actions may also damage a sense of authenticity and inhibit professional success.

It is crucial to stress that, although these difficulties are prominent, work is being made to overcome them. Organizations and people are increasingly understanding the value of diversity, inclusion, and equality, leading to efforts targeted at establishing more inclusive and fair workplaces for women. By increasing awareness, confronting preconceptions, campaigning for change, and supporting one another, women may overcome these barriers and contribute to a more inclusive and diverse workforce.

B. Strategies for establishing credibility and influence

Establishing credibility and influence is vital for women working in male-dominated areas. Here are some techniques that might assist in this regard:

1. Develop competence: Building a firm foundation of knowledge and competence in your subject is vital for building credibility. Continuously engage in learning and professional development to keep informed of industry trends, best practices, and new technology. Demonstrating knowledge through your work, study, and contributions may earn you the respect and confidence of your colleagues and superiors.

2. Seek Mentors and Sponsors: Mentors and sponsors may give essential direction, counsel, and assistance in navigating your profession and gaining influence. Look for people, both inside and outside your business, who have expertise and influence in your field. Engage in mentoring connections and pursue sponsorship possibilities to acquire recognition, access new prospects, and obtain advocacy for progress.

3. Network Strategically: Build a strong professional network by attending industry events, joining relevant organizations, and networking with peers and leaders in your sector. Network strategically by searching out people who can give important insights, guidance, and prospective partnerships. Actively engage in debates, offer your experience, and seek chances to exhibit your talents and accomplishments.

4. Communicate Effectively: Strong communication skills are vital for creating credibility and influence. Articulate your thoughts clearly, simply, and boldly. Listen intently to people and participate in meaningful discussions. Tailor your communication style to the audience, responding to diverse stakeholders and scenarios. Effectively convey your successes, ambitions, and vision to gather support and develop credibility.

5. Demonstrate outcomes: Delivering great outcomes and continually surpassing expectations is a powerful method to create credibility. Focus on high-quality work, fulfill deadlines, and go above and beyond your obligations. By continuously producing exceptional outputs, you will create a reputation for expertise and dependability, garnering the confidence and respect of others.

6. Build Relationships and Allies: Cultivate excellent relationships with colleagues, both inside and outside your business. Seek chances to cooperate, exchange expertise, and encourage one another. Building strong ties and allies may enhance your power and offer a support system through hard times. Engage in cross-functional initiatives, join employee resource groups, and engage in mentorship programs to broaden your network and develop relationships.

7. Be Confident and Assertive: Confidence and assertiveness play vital roles in creating credibility and influence. Believe in your strengths and worth, and exhibit confidence in your dealings. Assert yourself at meetings, talks, and negotiations, ensuring that your voice is heard and your ideas are considered. Speak out for yourself and others, questioning prejudices and fighting for inclusiveness.

8. Embrace exposure: Actively pursue exposure opportunities within your business and sector. Volunteer for high-profile initiatives, speak at conferences or industry events, and contribute to thought leadership by authoring articles or participating in panel discussions. Embracing exposure helps you exhibit your skills, build your network, and improve your impact.

Remember that creating credibility and influence is a constant process that involves persistence, self-belief, and proactive participation. By harnessing these methods, women may position themselves as important leaders, promoting good change and paving the way for future generations.

C. Building supportive networks and allies

Building supportive networks and allies is vital for personal and professional progress. Here are some techniques to help you develop such networks:

1. Identify Common hobbies: Look for people who have similar hobbies, beliefs, or professional objectives. This may be done by attending industry events, joining professional groups, participating in online forums, or engaging in networking activities inside your business. Seek out people who have a positive and collaborative outlook.

2. Cultivate Authentic ties: When constructing a network, concentrate on establishing real and meaningful ties. Take the time to get to know individuals on a personal level, expressing interest in their experiences, objectives, and difficulties. Be honest and real in your relationships, since people are more willing to support and advocate for individuals they trust and connect with.

3. Seek Mentors and Role Models: Mentors and role models may give you direction, counsel, and support as you navigate your profession. Look for people who have achieved success in your preferred sector or who have expertise in areas where you wish to expand. Approach them with a straightforward query and show your dedication to learning from their experiences. A mentor may give vital insights, help you overcome problems, and provide a larger perspective.

4. Participate in Employee Resource Groups (ERGs): Many firms offer Employee Resource

Groups (ERGs) or affinity groups that bring together individuals with common backgrounds, hobbies, or experiences. Joining these communities may give you a fantastic chance to interact with like-minded others, exchange experiences, and seek support. ERGs frequently provide networking events, professional development opportunities, and mentoring programs specifically for underrepresented groups.

5. Engage in Cross-Functional Projects: Collaborating on cross-functional projects enables you to engage with employees from other teams and departments within your firm. This gives you a chance to broaden your network outside your immediate circle and create ties with people who may have varied ideas and skills. Actively seek out these initiatives and share your talents and expertise.

6. Attend Networking Events: Attend industry conferences, seminars, workshops, and other networking events to meet people from all backgrounds and sectors. Engage in discussions, listen intently, and share contact information with people you connect with. Follow up with them later to foster the connection and investigate future partnership or mentoring options.

7. Give and Receive Support: Building a supportive network is a two-way street. Be willing to give support, advice, and aid to others when you can. Actively listen to their problems, give advice, and applaud their triumphs. By being supportive and helpful to others, you will create a reciprocal climate where others are more willing to provide support and assistance to you when required.

8. Utilize Online Platforms: Online platforms and social media may also be helpful tools for creating networks and finding supportive friends. Join professional groups on sites like LinkedIn, participate in important topics, and communicate with industry thought leaders. Share your skills and ideas via articles or posts to identify yourself as a useful addition to the community.

Remember, creating supportive networks and supporters takes time and effort. Be proactive in reaching out, building connections, and being a resource to others. By surrounding yourself with a supportive network, you may obtain essential advice, encouragement, and opportunities for development and success in your personal and professional paths.

CHAPTER 4: LEADERSHIP REDEFINED: PIONEERING WOMEN AT THE HELM

Leadership Redefined: Pioneering Women at the Helm refers to a concept that challenges conventional concepts of leadership and showcases the remarkable leadership abilities displayed by women in numerous disciplines. It honors the unique talents and views that women bring to leadership posts and their successes in breaking boundaries and leading with distinction.

In the past, leadership was generally linked with male attributes and hierarchical organizations. However, as more women have ascended to leadership roles, it has become obvious that good leadership transcends gender preconceptions and supports a more inclusive and varied approach.

A. Examining the leadership styles of pioneering women

Examining the leadership styles of pioneering women shows a varied variety of techniques and attributes that have led to their success. These women have bucked social expectations, burst through obstacles, and blazed trails in their respective areas. Here are some prominent leadership styles and attributes demonstrated by pioneering women:

1. Transformational Leadership: Many pioneering women demonstrate a transformational leadership style, distinguished by their capacity to inspire and drive others to attain their greatest potential. They build a common vision, inspire creativity, and enable their employees to thrive. By concentrating on individual growth and providing a supportive work environment, they promote significant change and produce outstanding outcomes.

2. Collaborative Leadership: Women's leaders generally promote cooperation and teamwork, acknowledging the significance of multiple viewpoints. They build inclusive settings where everyone's perspectives are heard, promoting a culture of open communication, trust, and respect. By exploiting the qualities and abilities of their people, they generate collective success and establish strong connections.

3. Authentic Leadership: Pioneering women frequently lead with honesty, staying true to their principles and convictions. They are straightforward, personable, and real, which helps them develop trust and form great ties with their employees. By being real, they inspire loyalty and generate a sense of purpose and meaning in their businesses.

4. Adaptive Leadership: Many pioneering women have proven the capacity to adjust to changing circumstances and manage challenging obstacles. They are robust, nimble, and quick to accept new ideas and technology. Their versatility helps them lead successfully in changing circumstances, fostering innovation and keeping ahead of the curve.

5. Empowering Leadership: Women leaders generally focus on empowering others and promoting a culture of mentoring and development. They give chances for skill development, provide advice and assistance, and establish avenues for progress. By fostering and empowering their staff, they build a sense of ownership and dedication, resulting in increased levels of engagement and achievement.

6. Socially Conscious Leadership: Pioneering women typically display a strong sense of social responsibility and utilize their leadership positions to advocate for good change. They encourage diversity and inclusion, promote social justice, and push environmental initiatives. Their socially aware leadership inspires others and helps create a more egalitarian and inclusive society.

It's crucial to highlight that leadership styles are not confined to gender, and these attributes may be demonstrated by leaders of either gender. However, evaluating the leadership styles of pioneering women emphasizes their distinct contributions and the influence they have had in breaking old standards and paving the way for future generations.

B. Impactful leadership traits and approaches

Impactful leadership features and tactics may vary based on the circumstances and individual preferences, but here are some common traits and approaches that are typically connected with successful leadership:

1. Vision and Purpose: Impactful leaders have a clear vision and a sense of purpose that inspire and drive their staff. They express a compelling direction and mobilize people behind a common objective, creating a sense of meaning and purpose in their work.

2. Strong Communication: Effective leaders are strong communicators who can explain their ideas and vision effectively and convincingly. They actively listen to others, create open communication, and give frequent feedback, ensuring that information flows easily across the business.

3. Empathy and Emotional Intelligence: Impactful leaders understand and sympathize with the emotions and experiences of their team members. They exhibit emotional intelligence, which helps them manage interpersonal dynamics, develop solid relationships, and resolve disputes successfully.

4. Decisiveness: Leaders need to make harsh choices and take action when required. They assess the available facts, examine diverse views, and make timely and well-informed decisions. Their decisiveness instills confidence and helps drive success.

5. Accountability: Impactful leaders hold themselves and others responsible for their actions and results. They set clear expectations, develop measures for success, and accept responsibility for their actions. They build a culture of ownership and honesty where people are inspired to achieve their best.

6. Continuous Learning: Effective leaders have a development attitude and promote continual learning. They explore chances for personal and professional growth, encourage their colleagues to do the same, and build a culture of inquiry and creativity.

7. Cooperation and Team Building: Impactful leaders appreciate the potential of cooperation and actively cultivate a feeling of teamwork. They establish an open and supportive atmosphere where varied opinions are appreciated, and they harness the capabilities of their team members to accomplish joint objectives.

8. Resilience and adaptation: Leaders experience obstacles and failures, but influential leaders display resilience and adaptation. They stay steady in the face of adversity, learn from setbacks, and change their plans as required. Their ability to handle change and uncertainty generates confidence in their teams.

9. Lead by Example: Impactful leaders lead by example, modeling the behaviors and values they demand from others. They display integrity, ethical conduct, and a strong work ethic. Their acts generate trust and serve as guidance for their staff.

10. Inspirational and Servant Leadership: Impactful leaders inspire and encourage people to attain their best potential. They coach and develop their team members, giving support and advice. They emphasize the development and well-being of their workers, producing a good and productive work environment.

These attributes and tactics may help leaders have a big and beneficial effect inside their businesses and beyond. However, it's crucial to remember that successful leadership is a constant journey of growth and development, and various circumstances may necessitate different leadership styles and techniques.

C. Case studies of successful women leaders in diverse industries

1. Indra Nooyi (Former CEO of PepsiCo): Indra Nooyi is internationally renowned for her successful term as the CEO of PepsiCo, a worldwide food and beverage business. She altered PepsiCo's product portfolio by emphasizing healthier alternatives and expanding into new markets. Nooyi's strategic leadership and dedication to sustainability made her a famous figure in the corporate world.

2. Mary Barra (Chair and CEO of General Motors): Mary Barra became the first female CEO of a major global automaker when she took leadership at General Motors (GM). Under her supervision, GM focused on innovation, customer-centricity, and technical improvements in the automobile sector. Barra's focus on building a culture of openness and accountability has been important to GM's success.

3. Ginni Rometty (Former CEO of IBM): Ginni Rometty headed IBM as CEO at a time of substantial transition in the technology sector. She played a crucial role in pushing IBM towards new technologies such as cloud computing, artificial intelligence, and data analytics. Rometty's strategic vision and focus on developing partnerships and alliances have positioned IBM as a leader in the digital age.

4. Sheryl Sandberg (COO of Facebook): Sheryl Sandberg is noted for her prominent job as the Chief Operating Officer of Facebook. She is an advocate for gender equality in the workplace and has published the book "Lean In," which encourages women to follow their objectives and overcome hurdles. Sandberg's leadership focuses on empowering people and encouraging innovation inside Facebook.

5. Ursula Burns (Former CEO of Xerox): Ursula Burns made history as the first African American woman to run a Fortune 500 corporation when she served as the CEO of Xerox. She managed Xerox through a hard era and successfully converted the firm into a diversified business services and technology organization. Burns is a champion for diversity and inclusion and has been recognized for her leadership in the business sector.

These women leaders have made important contributions to their respective professions, breaking boundaries and inspiring others with their leadership. Their success stories highlight the influence women can have as leaders in many sectors and serve as role models for aspiring leaders.

CHAPTER 5: EMPOWERING WOMEN: STRATEGIES FOR ADVANCEMENT AND SUCCESS

Empowering Women: Strategies for Advancement and Success focuses on empowering women with the skills and techniques they need to overcome barriers and accomplish their professional objectives. It analyzes numerous tactics and approaches that enable women to handle hurdles and develop a path to success. Some of these tactics include:

A. Building self-confidence and overcoming self-limiting beliefs

Building self-confidence and overcoming self-limiting beliefs are key stages in empowering oneself and attaining personal and professional progress. Here's an explanation of these concepts:

1. Building Self-Confidence: Building self-confidence entails creating a positive and realistic opinion of oneself and one's talents. It is a belief in one's worth, value, and potential to succeed. Here are some crucial factors in establishing self-confidence:

a. Recognizing strengths: Identifying and appreciating one's talents, abilities, and successes is vital for increasing confidence. Reflect on prior triumphs and acknowledge the distinctive traits and talents that led to success.

b. Setting feasible objectives: Setting realistic and achievable goals helps develop confidence gradually. Break huge ambitions into smaller, attainable activities, and celebrate each milestone along the way. Achieving these little objectives improves confidence and spurs future improvement.

c. Embracing a growth mentality: Adopting a growth mindset involves trusting in one's potential to learn, develop, and improve. Embrace problems as chances for progress rather than dreading failure. View failures as learning experiences and attempt to build new skills and information consistently.

d. Surrounding oneself with good influences: Surrounding oneself with helpful and encouraging folks who believe in one's skills may dramatically boost self-confidence. Seek out mentors, friends, or coworkers who give encouragement, support, and critical comments.

e. Taking care of oneself: Self-care plays a key role in developing self-confidence. Engage in activities that promote well-being, such as exercising, practicing mindfulness or meditation, pursuing hobbies, and maintaining a good work-life balance. Taking care of oneself promotes self-esteem and general confidence.

2. Overcoming Self-Limiting Beliefs: Self-limiting beliefs are negative ideas or assumptions that hold someone back from realizing their full potential. Overcoming these misconceptions is vital for personal development and opening new possibilities. Here are techniques to overcome self-limiting beliefs:

a. Identifying and addressing beliefs: Recognize and address self-limiting ideas that may be holding you back. Challenge the legitimacy and correctness of these ideas by obtaining evidence that disproves them. Replace negative thinking with positive and motivating affirmations.

b. Examining prior triumphs: Reflect on past successes and accomplishments to remind yourself of your strengths and potential. Use these prior triumphs as proof that problems can be overcome and objectives can be reached.

c. Seeking assistance and feedback: Seek support from trustworthy friends, mentors, or coaches who can give objective feedback and help question self-limiting beliefs. Often, an outside viewpoint may give a more balanced and realistic picture of one's talents and potential.

d. Taking calculated chances: Stepping beyond one's comfort zone and taking calculated risks might help one break free from self-imposed limits. Start with tiny steps, progressively pushing the limits of what seems comfortable. Each successful risk taken develops confidence and decreases self-limiting assumptions.

e. continual learning and growth: Engage in continual learning and skill development to enhance knowledge and capabilities. Acquiring new skills and information helps boost confidence and gives proof that growth and progress are possible.

Overcoming self-limiting attitudes and establishing self-confidence is a continuous process that takes self-reflection, tenacity, and a dedication to personal improvement. By questioning negative ideas, embracing strengths, and fostering a positive mentality, people may overcome hurdles, unleash their potential, and achieve greater success in all facets of life.

B. Negotiation skills and advocating for oneself

Negotiation skills and arguing for oneself are vital for personal and professional success. Here's an explanation of these concepts:

1. Negotiation Skills: Negotiation skills entail the capacity to communicate effectively, comprehend others' viewpoints, and develop mutually beneficial solutions in varied scenarios. Here are the major characteristics of bargaining skills:

a. Preparation: Before initiating a negotiation, it is necessary to acquire relevant information, identify clear objectives, and understand the interests and requirements of all parties involved. Being prepared empowers people to present their arguments confidently and make educated judgments.

b. Active listening and communication: Active listening entails carefully grasping the other party's concerns, needs, and goals. Effective communication abilities, such as clarity, empathy, and assertiveness, help explain one's perspective successfully and build a healthy discourse.

c. Problem-solving approach: Approach discussions with a problem-solving mindset rather than a win-lose mentality. Seek to discover innovative solutions that meet the interests of both parties, resulting in a mutually beneficial end.

d. Flexibility and compromise: Being open to compromise and finding common ground is crucial to effective negotiations. Flexibility in considering different choices and readiness to make sacrifices may assist in creating solutions that fulfill both sides' demands.

e. Confidence and assertiveness: Having confidence in one's skills, expressing thoughts and ideas assertively, and advocating for one's interests are crucial in negotiation. Confidence may be gained through preparation, education, and awareness of one's own value and worth.

2. Advocating for Oneself: Advocating for oneself means aggressively advocating one's interests, desires, and aspirations in personal and professional situations. Here are ways for successful self-advocacy:

a. Know your worth: Recognize and respect your abilities, achievements, and distinctive significance. Understand your abilities, knowledge, and the contributions you bring to the table.

b. Clearly articulate goals: Clearly identify your goals and objectives, both short-term and long-term. Communicate your ambitions to others, especially supervisors, coworkers, and mentors, so they can support and advocate for your achievement.

c. Self-promotion: Share your successes, accomplishments, and contributions with others. Don't be scared to mention your talents and triumphs when appropriate. Articulate your talents and experience in a strong and persuasive way.

d. pursue chances for growth: Actively pursue opportunities for professional development, skill upgrades, and promotion. Take initiative in seeking tough tasks or assignments that correspond with your objectives and exhibit your ability.

e. Build a support network: Cultivate connections with mentors, sponsors, and advocates who can give direction, support, and opportunities. These folks may give you guidance, suggest chances, and help magnify your voice and exposure.

f. Assertive communication: Practice assertive communication to convey your needs, limits, and thoughts clearly and respectfully. Learn to say "no" when required and bargain for resources, accolades, or chances that correspond with your objectives.

By acquiring negotiating skills and advocating for themselves, people may successfully navigate work situations, negotiate fair agreements, and aggressively pursue their objectives and desires. These talents contribute to personal development, job progress, and the formation of mutually beneficial relationships.

C. Mentorship and sponsorship opportunities for career growth

Mentorship and sponsorship are strong options for professional growth and development. Here's an explanation of these concepts:

1. Mentorship:

A mentor is a trustworthy and experienced person who offers direction, support, and counsel to a less experienced individual in their personal and professional growth. Here are the major components of mentorship:

a. Knowledge and Experience Sharing: Mentors offer their knowledge, expertise, and experiences to help mentees overcome problems, make informed choices, and build important skills for professional growth.

b. direction and Support: Mentors give direction and support by giving insights, comments, and constructive criticism. They assist mentees in developing objectives, identifying strengths and areas for improvement, and building action plans to achieve professional advancement.

c. Networking and Connections: Mentors may expose mentees to useful professional networks, link them with prominent people in their sector, and give them possibilities for exposure to new prospects and career routes.

d. Role Modeling: Mentors act as role models, influencing mentees through their achievements, leadership abilities, and ethical conduct. They exhibit the principles and actions important for professional success and assist mentees in building their own leadership styles.

e. Emotional Support: Mentors give emotional support, encouragement, and motivation during tough times. They act as a sounding board and provide a secure area for mentees to communicate worries, anxieties, and goals.

2. Sponsorship:
Sponsorship entails a senior-level professional advocating for and actively encouraging the career progress of a more junior individual within an organization or sector. Here are the major features of sponsorship:

a. Awareness and Advocacy: Sponsors utilize their power and position to establish awareness for their protégés inside the organization. They vigorously advocate for their protégés' talents, abilities, and potential, suggesting them for high-visibility initiatives, promotions, or leadership possibilities.

a. Opening Doors: Sponsors give access to key networks, powerful people, and career-enhancing possibilities that may not be readily available to their protégés. They provide avenues for progress and promote the protégés' professional growth.

c. Development and Feedback: Sponsors give direction, feedback, and development opportunities to help their protégés enhance their skill set, acquire experience, and overcome hurdles to promotion. They give constructive criticism and mentorship-like assistance to enhance the protégés' achievements.

c. Risk Mitigation: Sponsors are ready to assume measured risks on behalf of their protégés, vouching for their talents and potential. They assist in managing organizational politics, eliminating impediments, and creating a conducive atmosphere for the protégés' achievement.

d. Long-term Support: Sponsors are devoted to the long-term success of their protégés and continue to advocate for them throughout their careers. They celebrate their triumphs, give continuous support, and help them embrace new chances.

Mentorship and sponsorship connections may greatly affect an individual's professional trajectory by giving direction, support, opportunities, and access to key networks. Seeking out mentors and sponsors, both inside and beyond the workplace, may be crucial in speeding professional advancement, broadening networks, and opening doors to new opportunities.

CHAPTER 6: SHIFTING PARADIGMS: REDEFINING SUCCESS IN THE BUSINESS WORLD

Shifting Paradigms: Redefining Success in the Corporate World" is a notion that underlines the shifting perspectives and criteria of success within the corporate world. It understands the need to go beyond conventional measurements and adopt a more holistic and inclusive approach to defining and achieving success.

In the context of women in the corporate sector, "Shifting Paradigms" highlights the significance of breaking old gender stereotypes and overcoming hurdles that have traditionally hindered women's prospects for success. It attempts to build a more equitable and inclusive corporate environment that honors and promotes the progress of women.

One component of reframing success for women in business is shifting away from merely concentrating on traditional indicators like financial performance or hierarchical positions. While these variables are still significant, there is an emerging realization that success should incorporate a larger variety of criteria, such as work-life balance, personal growth, mentoring, leadership development, and social impact.

To redefine success for women in the business world, it is crucial to address several key areas:

1. Equal Opportunity: Shifting paradigms includes addressing structural obstacles that have traditionally disadvantaged women in the workplace. This involves supporting equitable access to education, training, and job progression opportunities, as well as combating unconscious prejudices and preconceptions.

2. Inclusive Leadership: Redefining success involves developing an inclusive and diverse leadership culture inside enterprises. It entails enabling women to pursue leadership positions and providing the necessary support and mentoring to enable them to succeed.

3. Work-Life Integration: Recognizing the varied character of women's lives, redefining success means fostering flexible work arrangements, family-friendly policies, and supportive workplaces that enable women to manage their professional and personal commitments.

4. Collaboration and mentoring: Shifting paradigms entails developing a culture of collaboration and mentoring where experienced professionals, both men and women, assist and encourage the career growth of women. This helps develop a network of support and provides possibilities for learning and growth.

5. Empowering Entrepreneurship: Redefining success also means promoting and supporting female entrepreneurs. This involves giving women access to money, mentoring programs, networking opportunities, and tools to help them begin and expand their enterprises.

By reframing success in the corporate sector with a focus on women, businesses may create a more inclusive and fair environment that benefits not just women but society as a whole. Embracing diversity and questioning established conventions leads to better creativity, smarter decision-making, and a more sustainable and productive economic environment.

A. Rethinking traditional measures of success

Rethinking traditional measurements of success requires examining and reassessing the customary metrics and criteria by which success is customarily judged. It understands that conventional metrics typically highlight certain characteristics of performance while omitting other key dimensions of success.

In many countries, success has historically been linked with things such as money, power, position, and material possessions. These outward signs of success have been profoundly embedded in our cultural and social narratives. However, there is a growing realization that this limited emphasis on outward indicators of success may be confining and fail to capture the whole range of human well-being and contentment.

Rethinking conventional measurements of success includes extending the viewpoint and contemplating a more holistic and multifaceted approach to evaluating personal and professional accomplishments. Here are some crucial elements to consider:

1. Well-being and Happiness: Success should not be only defined by financial affluence or professional prestige. It is necessary to regard individual well-being and pleasure as key components of success. Factors such as mental and physical health, work-life balance, and general life happiness should be given major weight in determining success.

2. Personal progress and Fulfillment: Success should entail personal progress and self-fulfillment. It entails continual learning, the growth of skills and abilities, following hobbies and interests, and accomplishing personal objectives. This component admits that success is a subjective and unique idea, ranging from person to person.

3. Relationships and ties: Meaningful relationships and social ties are vital to human well-being. Success may be assessed by the quality of relationships, the capacity to develop and sustain meaningful connections, and the influence one has on others' lives. This involves cultivating family relationships and friendships and contributing constructively to communities.

4. Effect and Contribution: Success may be judged by the positive effect one has on society and the globe at large. Making a difference, producing social change, and contributing to the improvement of others' lives may be regarded as key indicators of success. This may involve charity, advocacy, or efforts that solve social and environmental concerns.

5. Personal Values and sincerity: Success should coincide with personal values and sincerity. It comprises living in line with one's values and convictions, being genuine to oneself, and finding purpose and meaning in life and work. This element emphasizes that success cannot be determined only by external criteria but rather by individual beliefs and desires.

Rethinking conventional measurements of success provides for a more inclusive, balanced, and satisfying interpretation of performance. It recognizes that success is complex and varies among people, cultures, and settings. By widening the concept of success, people may pursue objectives and ambitions that are more aligned with their beliefs, leading to greater personal satisfaction and general well-being.

B. Embracing work-life integration and well-being

Embracing work-life integration and well-being is a concept that underlines the necessity of achieving a harmonic balance between work and personal life while emphasizing individual well-being. It emphasizes that conventional concepts of work-life balance sometimes create a split between professional and personal domains, making it hard for people, especially women, to manage their numerous roles and obligations efficiently.

In the context of pioneering women reinventing success in the corporate world, embracing work-life integration and well-being becomes vital. Here are some crucial things to explore:

1. Redefining Work-Life Integration: Work-life integration includes finding methods to effortlessly blend professional and personal elements of life, realizing that they are intertwined. It promotes flexibility, autonomy, and the capacity to integrate work and personal responsibilities in a manner that matches individual requirements and circumstances.

2. Shattering Gender Norms: Pioneering women defy established gender norms that typically impose a disproportionate responsibility on women to handle home and childcare tasks. By pushing for work-life integration, these women try to establish a more fair and inclusive work environment that supports the needs and goals of all people, regardless of their gender.

3. Flexible Work Arrangements: Embracing work-life integration means advocating and implementing flexible work arrangements. This includes choices like remote work, flexible hours, shortened workweeks, and job sharing, enabling workers to have more control over their schedules and meet personal responsibilities without sacrificing professional advancement.

4. Prioritizing Well-Being: Well-being involves physical, mental, and emotional health. Pioneering women in the corporate sector acknowledge the value of prioritizing self-care and well-being to preserve resilience, productivity, and overall contentment. This comprises supporting workplace practices that promote mental health, offering tools for stress management, and establishing a culture that prioritizes employee well-being.

5. Supportive Organizational Culture: Creating an organizational culture that fosters work-life integration and well-being is vital. This involves setting rules and procedures that create a healthy work environment, supporting open communication, providing resources for work-life balance, and offering support systems such as employee assistance programs and parental leave policies.

By embracing work-life integration and well-being, pioneering women in the business sector aspire to break down barriers and create a more inclusive and friendly work environment. They know that success should not come at the price of personal well-being and that achieving a balance between work and personal life is vital for overall pleasure and sustained professional advancement.

C. Championing diversity and inclusivity as markers of success

Championing diversity and inclusion as markers of success is a notion that emphasizes the value and relevance of promoting varied and inclusive settings within the corporate sector. It goes beyond standard measurements of success, such as financial performance or individual accomplishments, and stresses the larger effect and social responsibility of enterprises.

In the context of pioneering women redefining success in the corporate world, embracing diversity and inclusiveness becomes crucial. Here are some essential topics to explore:

1. Embracing Diversity: Pioneering women acknowledge that diversity spans a number of characteristics, including gender, color, ethnicity, age, sexual orientation, disability, and more. They encourage diversity by campaigning for fair representation and opportunity for people from varied backgrounds inside the workplace.

2. Building Inclusive Cultures: Inclusivity requires building a work environment where all employees feel appreciated, respected, and empowered to offer their unique ideas and experiences. Pioneering women develop inclusive environments by confronting prejudices, establishing a sense of belonging, and cultivating an atmosphere of cooperation and open-mindedness.

3. Leveraging various viewpoints: Pioneering women realize that various viewpoints contribute to innovation and improved decision-making. They advocate diversity and inclusion as indicators of success by actively seeking out and respecting other opinions, experiences, and ideas, realizing that they contribute to a more thorough understanding of complicated business situations.

4. Equal chances: Championing diversity and inclusion includes guaranteeing equal access to chances for professional growth, mentoring, and leadership development for people from all backgrounds. Pioneering women fight to demolish obstacles and prejudices that have traditionally restricted the growth of marginalized groups, establishing a more level playing field.

5. Social Impact and Duty: Pioneering women know that enterprises have a greater duty beyond financial success. They embrace diversity and inclusiveness as indicators of success by actively participating in social impact programs, supporting community development, and encouraging sustainable practices. This larger view of success takes into consideration the positive effect a company may have on society.

By embracing diversity and inclusiveness as indicators of success, pioneering women contribute to developing more inclusive, egalitarian, and socially responsible corporate settings. They acknowledge that diverse teams and inclusive environments stimulate innovation, boost company performance, and have a beneficial influence on society as a whole.ce organizational performance, and have a positive impact on society as a whole.

CHAPTER 7: FROM GLASS CEILING TO GLASS CLIFF: NAVIGATING CHALLENGES IN LEADERSHIP

"From Glass Ceiling to Glass Cliff: Navigating Problems in Leadership" is a concept that investigates the gender-related hurdles and problems that women encounter in obtaining leadership positions and the phenomenon known as the "glass cliff." It dives into the experiences of women in leadership positions and analyzes the particular challenges they confront while managing their professions.

1. Glass Ceiling: The glass ceiling refers to the unseen hurdles that prohibit women from progressing to top leadership positions in businesses. It depicts the systematic prejudices, gender preconceptions, and structural limits that hamper women's job growth despite their skills and talents.

2. Glass Cliff: The glass cliff phenomenon refers to the tendency that women are more likely to be selected for leadership roles during times of crisis or when businesses confront significant problems. This might expose them to greater degrees of risk and failure since they are typically expected to turn around tough situations or handle risky scenarios.

3. Navigating difficulties: The notion of navigating difficulties in leadership studies how women overcome the hurdles and prejudices they experience on their journey to leadership. It investigates techniques women utilize to manage gender-based challenges, build resilience, and acquire the required abilities to flourish in leadership positions.

4. Overcoming Bias: Women in leadership typically confront prejudices such as gender stereotypes, discrimination, and unconscious biases. Navigating obstacles includes actively confronting and removing these prejudices, developing gender-inclusive workplaces, and advocating equitable opportunity for women in leadership roles.

5. Leadership Development and Support: Navigating obstacles necessitates giving women access to leadership development programs, mentoring, and sponsorship opportunities. Offering support networks and tools may help women grow confidence, enhance their abilities, and overcome the barriers they confront.

6. Creating Inclusive Companies: To break the glass barrier and handle problems successfully, it is vital to develop inclusive companies that encourage diversity, give equitable chances, and provide supportive environments. This involves enacting rules that encourage work-life integration, flexible work arrangements, and family-friendly programs.

7. Creating knowledge and Advocacy: Navigating obstacles in leadership entails creating knowledge of the glass ceiling, the glass cliff, and gender biases in the workplace. Advocacy initiatives strive to stimulate conversation, push change, and urge organizations and people to actively work for gender equality and inclusion.

By addressing the concept of the glass ceiling and the challenges women face in leadership roles, "From Glass Ceiling to Glass Cliff: Navigating Challenges in Leadership" highlights the need for systemic change, increased representation, and supportive environments to ensure equal opportunities for women in leadership positions. It strives to equip women to handle the problems they experience and promote a more equal and inclusive future for everyone.

A. Exploring the phenomenon of the glass cliff

The glass cliff phenomenon refers to the pattern where women are more likely to be nominated for leadership roles during times of crisis or when businesses confront significant problems. This phrase was created by scholars Michelle K. Ryan and Alex Haslam in 2005, expanding upon the notion of the glass ceiling.

The glass cliff is seen in different spheres, including politics, business, and other organizational environments. It emphasizes the trend of women being nominated for leadership jobs when the possibility of failure or risk is high. This might include events such as taking over faltering enterprises, heading organizations suffering financial downturns, or assuming leadership amid periods of instability or war.

Several causes contribute to the glass cliff phenomenon:

115

1. Perceptions of Risk-Taking: There is a view that women exhibit certain attributes, such as empathy, cooperation, and risk aversion, that make them well-suited to handle crises. This impression might lead to their appointment when the risks and difficulties are considerable.

2. Stereotypes and Expectations: Gender stereotypes may impact the expectations put on women leaders. They may be expected to thrive in adverse conditions, attributed the position of "fixer" or "savior," or loaded with the obligation to turn the organization's fortunes around.

3. Availability and Opportunity: During times of crisis, organizations may broaden their pool of possible leaders to include women owing to a limited number of competent or interested male candidates. This may offer opportunities for women to take on leadership roles that may have been inaccessible in more stable settings.

4. Confirmation Bias: The glass cliff may be perpetuated through confirmation bias when the failures or problems experienced by women leaders in adverse circumstances are more likely to be recalled and generalized. This might foster the idea that women are fundamentally less adept at leadership jobs.

The glass cliff creates specific hurdles for female leaders. They may endure harsh scrutiny, higher demands, and fewer support networks compared to their male colleagues. They may also confront increased opposition and distrust, making it more difficult to excel in their professions.

However, it is crucial to emphasize that not all women nominated for leadership jobs during hard times will suffer failure. Many women have successfully negotiated the glass cliff and accomplished tremendous successes, breaking preconceptions and paving the way for future generations of women leaders.

Addressing the glass cliff problem demands efforts to eradicate gender biases and preconceptions in leadership selection procedures. Organizations may strive towards fostering inclusive environments, supporting support networks, and providing equitable opportunities for women to lead in both stressful and stable conditions. By building a more fair and supportive workplace, the glass ceiling may be reduced, enabling women leaders to flourish and contribute successfully to corporate success.

B. Strategies for overcoming challenges in leadership roles

Overcoming problems in leadership jobs involves a mix of personal tactics and structural assistance. Here are some ways that might help people navigate and overcome obstacles in leadership:

1. Build a Support Network: Cultivate a strong support network of mentors, coaches, and peers who can give direction, counsel, and encouragement. Seek out people who have had similar issues and may offer insights and support along the journey.

2. Develop Emotional Intelligence: Emotional intelligence entails understanding and controlling one's own emotions and those of others. It is vital for good leadership. By cultivating emotional intelligence, leaders can handle challenging circumstances, form connections, and inspire and drive their people.

3. Ongoing Learning and Skill Development: Embrace a growth mindset and commit to ongoing learning and skill development. Stay informed with industry trends, seek out professional development opportunities, and learn new information and skills that are relevant to your leadership job.

4. Foster Resilience: Resilience is the capacity to bounce back from setbacks and adapt to obstacles. Cultivate resilience by having a positive mentality, practicing self-care, and establishing ways to deal with stress. Embrace failures as learning opportunities and consider obstacles as stepping stones towards progress.

5. Seek input and Learn from Mistakes: Actively seek input from coworkers, team members, and supervisors. Embrace constructive criticism and learn from errors. Reflect on prior experiences and utilize them as chances for development and advancement.

6. Advocate for Yourself: Be aggressive in advocating for yourself and your ideas. Communicate your successes, talents, and goals to others, particularly supervisors and decision-makers. Take responsibility for your job path and aggressively explore possibilities for development and progress.

7. Build a varied and Inclusive Team: Surround yourself with a varied team that contributes a diversity of viewpoints, experiences, and abilities. Create an inclusive workplace where everyone feels respected and encouraged to offer their best. Embrace variety and exploit the abilities of each team member.

8. Develop Effective Communication Skills: Effective communication is crucial for effective leadership. Hone your communication abilities, both verbal and non-verbal, to explain your ideas, inspire people, handle issues, and develop great connections. Active listening and clear, precise communication are necessary.

9. Balance Priorities and Delegate: Prioritize tasks and responsibilities based on their significance and effect. Recognize that you cannot accomplish everything on your own and learn to delegate successfully. Empower and trust your team members to take responsibility for their responsibilities and contribute to the overall success of the business.

10. Maintain Work-Life Integration: Strive for work-life integration rather than tight isolation. Set limits, manage time wisely, and prioritize self-care. Recognize that a good work-life balance adds to overall well-being and promotes leadership effectiveness.

These tactics may enable people to handle hurdles in leadership positions and create personal and professional success. It is crucial to adjust and customize these methods to individual circumstances, company culture, and particular problems experienced in your leadership path.

C. Creating support systems for women in leadership positions

Creating solid support structures for women in leadership roles is vital for their success and progress. Here are some strategies to consider:

1. Mentorship and Sponsorship Programs: Establish official mentorship and sponsorship programs that link women leaders with seasoned professionals who can give guidance, counsel, and advocacy. Mentors may give professional insights, share their experiences, and provide significant networking opportunities, while sponsors actively advocate for and support women leaders inside the business.

2. Leadership Development Activities: Implement leadership development activities geared exclusively for women in leadership roles. These programs might concentrate on skill-building, executive coaching, and addressing the special obstacles and prejudices that women confront. Offer workshops, seminars, and training sessions to increase leadership abilities and empower women leaders.

3. Networking and Community Building: Foster networking opportunities and develop communities where women leaders may interact, exchange experiences, and support one another. This might involve creating events, seminars, or affinity clubs that bring together women executives from varied backgrounds and sectors.

4. Flexible Work Arrangements: Provide flexible work arrangements to enable women leaders to balance their professional and personal commitments. Flexible hours, remote work choices, and alternate scheduling may help with work-life integration and boost retention and productivity.

5. Equal Pay and Promotion Policies: Ensure pay fairness and adopt clear promotion processes that prevent gender prejudice. Conduct frequent salary audits and fix any irregularities. Promote a culture of fairness and meritocracy where women leaders have equal opportunity for professional progression and recognition.

6. Employee Resource Groups: Establish employee resource groups (ERGs) or affinity groups focused on assisting women in leadership roles. These groups may offer a forum for women to exchange ideas, solve common difficulties, and advocate for gender equality in the workplace.

7. Bias Awareness and Training: Conduct bias awareness and unconscious bias training for all workers, especially supervisors and leaders. Create awareness about the prejudices that might hinder women's progress and empower personnel with skills to avoid bias in decision-making processes.

8. Transparent Performance Evaluation Processes: Implement objective and open performance evaluation systems that guarantee a fair appraisal of women leaders. Provide frequent feedback, reward successes, and offer opportunities for growth and development.

9. Professional-Life Integration Support: Offer tools and support systems that help women leaders combine their professional and home lives efficiently. This might include offering access to daycare facilities, family-friendly policies, and support for handling work-life difficulties.

10. Executive Commitment and Accountability: Ensure that senior executives and organizational leaders exhibit commitment to gender equality and the support of women in leadership. Hold leaders responsible for establishing inclusive and supportive cultures and frequently monitor progress toward gender diversity targets.

By building complete support structures, businesses may empower women leaders, encourage their career progression, and create an inclusive and diverse leadership pipeline. It is crucial to include leaders at all levels, establish a culture of gender equality, and regularly analyze and adjust support efforts based on the shifting requirements of women in leadership roles.

CHAPTER 8: CHAMPIONING CHANGE: CREATING GENDER-INCLUSIVE WORKPLACES

Championing Change: Creating Gender-Inclusive Workplaces is the active promotion and advocacy for converting workplaces into settings that welcome and encourage gender equality. It comprises taking a proactive attitude in pushing change to eradicate gender prejudices, discrimination, and injustices and building a work culture where all people, regardless of their gender, have equal chances, rights, and recognition.

Championing change requires identifying the current hurdles and problems that inhibit gender inclusion within companies and taking purposeful measures to solve them. It involves actively working towards creating an atmosphere where women and other underrepresented genders may flourish and achieve, and where their contributions and perspectives are appreciated and respected.

Creating gender-inclusive workplaces entails establishing policies, programs, and practices that provide equitable access to opportunities, fair treatment, and representation at all levels of the business. It involves encouraging diversity in recruiting and hiring, offering equal remuneration and benefits, facilitating work-life integration, developing inclusive leadership and decision-making, and building a culture of respect and inclusiveness.

By promoting change and building gender-inclusive workplaces, firms contribute to a more fair society, boost employee well-being and happiness, unleash the full potential of their workforce, and promote innovation and success. It is an ongoing commitment that involves continual effort, education, awareness, and responsibility to achieve permanent change and demolish gender-related obstacles inside the workplace.

A. Implementing policies and initiatives to promote gender equality

Implementing laws and measures to promote gender equality is vital for fostering inclusive workplaces and guaranteeing equal opportunity for all workers. Here are some major policies and actions that companies might consider:

1. Gender Pay Equity: Conduct frequent pay audits to detect and correct any gender pay inequalities within the business. Ensure that women get equal pay for equal effort and ensure transparency in payment systems. Establish clear principles for fair pay practices, and frequently examine and improve them.

2. Diverse Recruitment and Hiring Practices: Implement tactics to recruit and employ a diverse pool of talent. This includes utilizing gender-neutral job descriptions and criteria, increasing recruiting channels to reach a larger audience, and employing diverse interview panels to prevent prejudice. Set diversity targets and constantly assess progress to guarantee responsibility.

3. Flexible Work Arrangements: Offer flexible work arrangements, such as flexible hours, remote work choices, and part-time or job-sharing possibilities. These programs encourage work-life integration for all workers and help relieve gender-specific issues linked to caregiving and job duties.

4. Parental Leave and Family-Friendly Policies: Establish comprehensive parental leave rules that give equal opportunity for both moms and dads to take time off to care for their children. Offer family-friendly policies, such as on-site daycare facilities or subsidies, breastfeeding spaces, and flexible return-to-work programs.

5. Leadership Development and Mentoring Programs: Implement leadership development programs and mentorship efforts that explicitly concentrate on supporting and encouraging women's professional growth. Provide training, mentoring, and networking opportunities to assist women in acquiring the skills and networks essential for leadership roles.

6. Unconscious Bias Training: Conduct frequent training sessions on unconscious bias awareness for workers at all levels. Raise awareness of biases that might affect decision-making processes, including hiring, promotions, and performance reviews. Provide tools and techniques to minimize prejudice and promote fair and objective decision-making.

7. Employee Resource Groups: Establish employee resource groups or affinity groups focusing on gender equality and women's empowerment. These organizations provide a venue for workers to share experiences, give support, and advocate for gender equality measures inside the firm.

8. Mentorship and Sponsorship Programs: Create formal mentorship and sponsorship programs that link women with seasoned professionals who can give direction, support, and advocacy. Encourage both women and men to engage in these activities to promote a culture of support and development.

9. Transparent Performance Evaluation and Promotion Processes: Implement open and fair performance assessment and promotion systems. Set explicit criteria and standards for assessments, and ensure that they are implemented uniformly across all workers. Provide frequent feedback and opportunities for professional advancement.

10. Accountability and Measurement: Establish metrics and routinely assess progress toward gender equality targets. Hold leaders and managers responsible for establishing and supporting inclusive and equitable practices. Review and adjust policies and activities based on feedback and data to constantly improve and solve gaps.

By adopting these policies and programs, companies may create a more inclusive and equitable work environment, attract and retain diverse talent, and establish a culture that appreciates and encourages gender equality. It takes a comprehensive strategy that incorporates policy, training, leadership commitment, and constant monitoring to generate effective change.

B. Creating inclusive cultures that support women's advancement

Creating inclusive cultures that assist women's progress entails establishing an atmosphere where women are empowered, appreciated, and given equal chances for growth and development. Here are crucial factors for developing such inclusive cultures:

1. Equal Opportunity and Representation: Ensure that women have equal access to chances for growth, including leadership roles, difficult projects, and professional development programs. Strive for gender-balanced representation at all levels of the organization to foster varied viewpoints and experiences.

2. Empowerment and Encouragement: Encourage women's involvement, contributions, and leadership by building a supportive and inclusive workplace. Provide them with the tools, coaching, and sponsorship required to increase their talents, acquire confidence, and take on significant positions.

3. Flexible Work Practices: Implement flexible work arrangements that facilitate work-life integration, enabling women to juggle their professional and personal duties efficiently. This might include flexible hours, remote work opportunities, and supportive policies for parental leave and caregiving.

4. Training and Development: Offer personalized training and development programs that meet the particular requirements and problems experienced by women. This might include leadership development efforts, negotiating skills training, and mentoring programs that provide women with the required skills and knowledge for job growth.

5. Addressing Unconscious Bias: Educate workers about unconscious biases and their influence on decision-making processes. Create knowledge and give tools to eliminate biases in recruiting, performance reviews, and promotions, guaranteeing a fair and impartial process for all workers.

6. Inclusive Communication and Collaboration: Promote inclusive communication methods that enable women to voice their thoughts, ideas, and concerns without fear of judgment or marginalization. Foster a collaborative and courteous work atmosphere that honors varied opinions and fosters open debate.

7. Recognition and Rewards: Ensure that women's efforts and accomplishments are recognized and appreciated. Implement fair and open incentive systems that appreciate their performance and give them equitable opportunities for promotion and growth.

8. Workforce Support and Well-Being: Provide support structures and resources that emphasize employee well-being. This might include mental health programs, flexible benefits, employee help programs, and measures to alleviate work-related stress and burnout.

9. Accountability and Measurement: Hold leaders and managers responsible for building and nurturing an inclusive culture that promotes women's growth. Establish measurements and frequently monitor progress towards gender equality targets to guarantee continual growth.

10. Collaboration with Employee Resource Groups: Collaborate with employee resource groups or affinity groups focusing on gender equality and women's growth. Seek feedback, participate in debate, and work together to solve obstacles and adopt initiatives that enhance women's professional growth.

Creating inclusive environments that promote women's growth takes a multi-faceted strategy that incorporates changes in rules, procedures, and attitudes. It entails establishing a culture of respect, equality, and empowerment where everyone is acknowledged for their efforts and given equal opportunity to thrive and develop in their professions.

C. Fostering diversity and inclusion at all levels of the organization

Fostering diversity and inclusion at all levels of the company involves building an atmosphere that appreciates and supports people from varied backgrounds, opinions, and experiences. It requires ensuring that everyone feels included, appreciated, and empowered to share their unique abilities and viewpoints. Here's an explanation of how to create diversity and inclusion at all levels:

1. Leadership Commitment: Leadership plays a critical role in developing diversity and inclusion. It begins with a clear commitment from senior leadership to promote diversity and inclusion as key principles of the firm. Leaders should actively support and promote diversity, set the example for inclusive behaviors, and hold themselves and others responsible for fostering an inclusive culture.

2. Diverse Recruitment and Hiring: Implement tactics to recruit and employ diverse talent. This involves extending recruiting channels, employing diverse interview panels, and aggressively seeking out people from underrepresented groups. Review and modify job descriptions and criteria to ensure they are inclusive and balanced.

3. Inclusive Policies and Procedures: Review and update organizational policies and procedures to ensure they are inclusive and promote equality. This covers rules on recruiting, promotion, remuneration, perks, and employee development. Eliminate any prejudices or impediments that hamper the progress of people from varied backgrounds.

4. Bias knowledge and Training: Provide training programs that improve knowledge regarding unconscious biases and their influence on decision-making processes. Equip workers at all levels with tools and tactics to eliminate prejudice in recruiting, performance assessments, and daily interactions.

5. Inclusive Leadership Development: Implement leadership development programs that promote inclusive leadership competencies. Provide training and mentoring to leaders to strengthen their capacity to establish an inclusive atmosphere, manage diverse teams successfully, and promote equitable chances for development and progress.

6. Employee Resource Groups: Support and promote the development of employee resource groups or affinity groups that concentrate on encouraging diversity and inclusion. These organizations provide a venue for workers to interact, exchange stories, and push for change. Collaborate with these organizations to solve particular concerns and build activities that enhance inclusiveness.

7. Mentorship and Sponsorship: Establish mentorship and sponsorship programs that link people from varied backgrounds with experienced professionals who can give advice, support, and advocacy. Encourage leaders to act as mentors and sponsors for people who may encounter impediments to progress.

8. Inclusive Communication and Collaboration: Foster an inclusive communication culture where all workers feel comfortable sharing their perspectives and ideas. Encourage active listening, seek varied viewpoints, and give chances for open debate and cooperation across all levels of the company.

9. Performance Evaluation and Recognition: Ensure that performance evaluations are fair, transparent, and free from prejudice. Evaluate workers based on their abilities, accomplishments, and contributions rather than on prejudices or personal biases. Recognize and appreciate varied skills and achievements to foster an inclusive culture.

10. Ongoing Measurement and Evaluation: Regularly evaluate progress towards diversity and inclusion objectives and track important indicators. Conduct employee surveys, gather feedback, and utilize data to analyze the organization's inclusion and find areas for improvement.

By cultivating diversity and inclusion at all levels of the company, firms may leverage the value of varied viewpoints, experiences, and abilities. This leads to enhanced innovation, creativity, and flexibility, as well as better employee engagement, satisfaction, and retention. It fosters an atmosphere where people may grow, offer their best, and realize their greatest potential.

CHAPTER 9: THE NEXT GENERATION: EMPOWERING FUTURE WOMEN LEADERS

The Next Generation: Empowering Future Women Leaders" refers to the attention and devotion to developing and inspiring young women to become future leaders. It entails offering people the tools, resources, support, and chances essential to improving their leadership abilities, creating confidence, and overcoming challenges they may experience in their professional paths.

Empowering future women leaders requires building an atmosphere that encourages girls and young women to discover their potential, follow their interests, and imagine themselves as effective leaders in diverse sectors. It requires breaking down cultural conventions and preconceptions that restrict their goals and giving them equal access to education, mentoring, and job development opportunities.

By developing future female leaders, we pave the way for a more equal and inclusive society. It not only helps individual women individually but also contributes to the broader growth, innovation, and well-being of communities and countries. It needs a joint effort from people, educational institutions, organizations, and legislators to create an enabling climate where young women may grow, lead, and make a good effect on the world.

A. Nurturing leadership skills in young girls and women

Nurturing leadership qualities in young girls and women means supporting their development, confidence, and ability to become successful leaders. It focuses on providing people with the appropriate support, opportunity, and resources to build and grow their leadership talents. Here are some crucial characteristics for cultivating leadership qualities in young girls and women:

1. Education and Skill Development: Offer educational programs and activities that promote leadership development. Provide access to training, seminars, and courses that enhance abilities such as communication, critical thinking, problem-solving, decision-making, and cooperation. By training girls and women with these core abilities, they may build the essential tools to lead successfully.

2. Mentorship and Role Models: Connect young girls and women with mentors and role models who can give guidance, counsel, and support. Mentors may share their own leadership experiences, give support, and act as a source of inspiration. Having role models who have successfully navigated leadership responsibilities may help young girls and women imagine their own potential as leaders.

3. Building Confidence and Self-Esteem: Encourage young girls and women to believe in themselves and their potential. Provide chances for them to take on leadership responsibilities, participate in public speaking, and engage in activities that enhance their self-confidence. Creating a secure and supportive atmosphere where people can express themselves without fear of criticism is vital for their development as leaders.

4. Promoting Resilience and Risk-Taking: Teach young girls and women the significance of resilience and the capacity to bounce back from obstacles and setbacks. Encourage them to take chances, move out of their comfort zones, and embrace possibilities for development. Building resilience helps individuals negotiate obstacles, learn from experiences, and continue in their leadership journeys.

5. Encouraging Collaboration and Teamwork: Emphasize the benefits of collaboration and teamwork in leadership. Foster an atmosphere where girls and women can work together, exchange ideas, and learn from one another. Provide chances for group projects, team-building exercises, and community participation to enhance their abilities in cooperation and consensus-building.

6. Empowering Decision-Making: Encourage young girls and women to take initiative and make choices. Provide them with the opportunity to lead initiatives, make decisions, and be responsible for their actions. By enabling students to make choices, they build confidence and acquire important leadership qualities.

7. Creating secure areas for Expression: Establish secure and inclusive areas where girls and women may freely express themselves and their opinions. Encourage children to express their thoughts, ask questions, and participate in productive debate. By providing an atmosphere that honors their viewpoints, students may enhance their communication and leadership abilities.

8. Providing Leadership chances: Offer numerous leadership chances, both within school settings and community groups. This may involve acting as class reps, participating in student councils, joining clubs or groups, and volunteering for leadership positions. Actively seek out and provide chances for young girls and women to display their leadership qualities.

9. Promoting Diversity and Inclusion: Emphasize the value of diversity and inclusion in leadership. Encourage young girls and women to embrace diversity, appreciate other ideas, and actively seek chances to lead in varied contexts. By recognizing and accepting various viewpoints, they establish inclusive leadership styles that reflect the needs and experiences of a wider spectrum of individuals.

10. Ongoing Support and Encouragement: Continuously give support, encouragement, and acknowledgment to young girls and women in their leadership journeys. Celebrate their triumphs, appreciate their efforts, and give constructive comments for improvement. Create a supportive network that fosters their leadership potential.

Nurturing leadership abilities in young girls and women is vital for building a new generation of empowered and effective leaders. By investing in their development, we not only unleash their potential but also help develop a more equal and inclusive society where various views are heard and appreciated.

B. Educational initiatives and mentorship programs

Educational initiatives and mentoring programs play a significant role in promoting the growth, development, and success of people, especially in the context of cultivating leadership abilities. Here's an explanation of these two components:

149

1. Educational Initiatives: Educational initiatives refer to programs, events, and resources meant to increase knowledge, skills, and personal growth. In the context of leadership development, educational efforts might include:

a. Leadership Development Programs: Structured programs that provide participants with particular information, skills, and experiences linked to leadership These programs may include workshops, seminars, courses, or experiential learning opportunities focusing on leadership theories, communication, decision-making, problem-solving, and other pertinent skills.

b. Skill-Building Workshops: Workshops that target particular leadership qualities such as public speaking, conflict resolution, team management, strategic thinking, and emotional intelligence These programs provide practical skills and approaches that people may implement in their leadership responsibilities.

c. Personal Development Training: Programs that concentrate on building self-awareness, self-confidence, resilience, and other personal traits important for successful leadership These programs frequently involve exercises like self-reflection, goal-setting, and attitude development.

d. Industry-certain Training: Educational efforts geared to certain industries or sectors provide people with knowledge and skills appropriate to leadership positions in such domains. This may include programs that concentrate on sector-specific difficulties, laws, or best practices.

e. Online Learning Platforms: Utilizing online platforms and resources to offer instructional material, such as leadership courses, webinars, and e-learning modules These platforms give users flexibility in accessing educational resources and allow them to study at their own pace.

2. Mentorship Programs: Mentorship programs entail linking people with experienced professionals who act as mentors, giving advice, support, and information exchange. In the context of leadership development, mentoring programs may offer:

a. Role Modeling: Mentors act as role models by showing good leadership behaviors and sharing their personal experiences and insights. They inspire and encourage mentees by displaying successful leadership routes and enabling mentees to visualize their own prospects.

b. Guidance and advice: Mentors give guidance and advice based on their experiences and skills. They give unique ideas, viewpoints, and practical advice on numerous elements of leadership, career development, and personal improvement.

c. Skill Development: Mentors support mentees in improving certain leadership abilities, such as communication, decision-making, and networking. They may create chances for mentees to practice and enhance these abilities, giving constructive criticism and support along the way.

d. Support and Encouragement: Mentors give emotional support, encouragement, and comfort to mentees, especially during hard times or when confronting hurdles. They provide a secure area for mentees to voice issues, seek direction, and get affirmation.

e. Networking and Connections: Mentors may assist mentees in extending their professional networks by offering introductions, creating connections, and organizing chances for mentees to interact with significant people in their particular areas.

Both educational efforts and mentoring programs are key components of leadership development since they complement each other in offering a thorough and holistic learning experience. Educational efforts provide people with the knowledge, skills, and theoretical underpinnings of leadership, while mentoring programs give practical assistance, support, and real-world insights from experienced leaders. Together, these projects and programs contribute to the growth and development of aspiring leaders, helping them to prosper and make a good influence in their chosen sectors.

C. Encouraging entrepreneurship and innovation among women

Encouraging entrepreneurship and innovation among women requires building an atmosphere that encourages and enables women to explore entrepreneurial enterprises and contribute to creative solutions. It strives to tear down barriers and promote equitable opportunities for women to establish and build their own enterprises, as well as boost their involvement in innovation-driven sectors. Here's an explanation of how to boost entrepreneurship and creativity among women:

1. Education and Skills Development: Provide access to entrepreneurial education, training, and skill-building programs that empower women with the knowledge and abilities required to establish and run firms. This covers classes on entrepreneurship, business planning, financial management, marketing, and leadership skills development. By strengthening their business acumen and entrepreneurial perspective, women are better equipped to negotiate the hurdles of entrepreneurship and create innovation.

2. Mentorship and Networking: Establish mentorship programs that link prospective women entrepreneurs with established entrepreneurs, company leaders, or industry experts who can give assistance, share ideas, and provide support. Mentors may give vital advice, assist in navigating the business environment, and inspire confidence in women to follow their entrepreneurial dreams. Networking activities, such as business gatherings, conferences, and industry groups, can also be promoted to create relationships and access to resources.

3. Access to Cash and Financial Support: Increase access to cash and financial resources for women entrepreneurs. This might entail giving microloans, grants, venture capital, or other financial choices particularly geared to helping women-led companies. Financial institutions, government initiatives, and angel investor networks may play a significant role in providing essential financial assistance to women entrepreneurs, helping them overcome the conventional hurdles to getting finance.

4. Promoting Role Models and Success Stories: Highlight successful women entrepreneurs and their accomplishments as role models. Sharing success stories and presenting varied instances of women-led firms may motivate other women to pursue entrepreneurship and innovation. It helps overcome gender stereotypes and fosters the concept that women can flourish as entrepreneurs and innovators in numerous fields.

5. Creating Supportive Entrepreneurial Ecosystems: Foster supportive ecosystems that offer the essential infrastructure, resources, and networks for women entrepreneurs. This comprises incubators, accelerators, co-working spaces, and company development centers that give access to mentoring, business support services, technical aid, and networking opportunities. Collaboration with industry groups, chambers of commerce, and entrepreneurial organizations may assist in building an enabling climate for women entrepreneurs.

6. Addressing Cultural and Societal hurdles: Tackle cultural and societal hurdles that may discourage or restrict women's engagement in entrepreneurship and innovation. This entails addressing gender prejudices, promoting gender equality, and pushing for legislation and programs that promote work-life balance, maternity and paternity leave, and equitable opportunity for women in the business environment.

7. Recognition and Awards: Recognize and celebrate the accomplishments of women entrepreneurs and inventors via awards and recognition programs. Acknowledging their accomplishments not only enhances their confidence and exposure but also motivates other women to seek entrepreneurial pathways and contribute to innovation.

8. Collaboration and Knowledge Sharing: Foster collaboration and knowledge sharing among women entrepreneurs and inventors. Encourage the establishment of networks, groups, and platforms where women may interact, exchange ideas, share experiences, and cooperate on initiatives. This relationship supports collaborative learning, enhances the effect of women-led companies, and stimulates innovation via varied viewpoints.

By fostering entrepreneurship and creativity among women, nations may unleash a wealth of untapped potential and promote economic progress. It empowers women to establish their own chances, contribute to employment development, and provide new ideas and answers to social concerns. Embracing and supporting women's entrepreneurial goals leads to a more inclusive and diversified entrepreneurial environment, benefiting people, communities, and economies as a whole.

CHAPTER 10: BEYOND BUSINESS: PIONEERING WOMEN MAKING A SOCIAL IMPACT

Beyond Business: Pioneering Women Making a Social Impact" refers to a concept or topic that focuses on women who are not only successful in their professional efforts but also devoted to producing good social change and making a difference in their communities and the globe. It celebrates the efforts and successes of women who go beyond typical commercial aims and utilize their talents, resources, and influence to solve social, environmental, or humanitarian concerns.

This notion highlights that women have a distinct viewpoint and set of experiences that may help solve numerous societal challenges and promote lasting change. It promotes the concept that success extends beyond financial benefits and involves the effects and good consequences women may have through their activities and ideas.

The notion of "Beyond Business: Pioneering Women Making a Social Impact" honors women who utilize their abilities, resources, and influence to contribute constructively to society. It recognizes their efforts to generate lasting change, promote social justice, and make a real impact in the lives of others. By recognizing and magnifying their efforts, this idea intends to inspire others, challenge conventional views of success, and encourage more women to participate in projects that generate social impact alongside their corporate pursuits.

Beyond Business: Pioneering Women Making a Social Impact" may comprise a broad variety of undertakings and projects performed by women, such as:

A. Exploring how pioneering women contribute to societal change

Pioneering women play a significant role in promoting social change through their inventive thinking, perseverance, and devotion to having a good influence. There are many ways in which pioneering women contribute to cultural change:

1. Breaking Obstacles and Challenging Gender Norms: Pioneering women defy society's norms and prejudices by breaking through obstacles and joining historically male-dominated areas. Their successes inspire and motivate other women, altering cultural ideas of what women can do.

2. Leadership and Representation: Pioneering women in leadership roles serve as role models and catalysts for change. Their presence in powerful capacities helps transform corporate cultures, policies, and practices to be more inclusive and gender-responsive. By pushing for diversity and inclusion, they help to tear down structural obstacles and generate possibilities for others.

3. Advocacy and Activism: Pioneering women typically utilize their platforms and power to campaign for social justice, gender equality, and human rights. They raise awareness about crucial problems, challenge unfair behaviors, and press for governmental reforms that alleviate social inequities.

4. Entrepreneurship and Social Innovation: Pioneering women influence societal change via entrepreneurial initiatives and social innovation. They build enterprises and organizations that solve social, environmental, or humanitarian concerns, promoting economic growth, providing employment opportunities, and supporting sustainable development.

5. Philanthropy and Charitable Work: Pioneering women contribute to cultural transformation via charitable initiatives. They utilize their financial resources, influence, and networks to assist causes and organizations that solve urgent social concerns, such as poverty reduction, education, healthcare, environmental conservation, and gender equality.

6. Education and mentoring: Pioneering women typically play a vital role in education and mentoring. They empower and inspire the next generation by sharing their expertise, experiences, and ideas. By fostering and supporting the development of young women and girls, they contribute to developing a pipeline of future leaders and changemakers.

7. Policy and Governance: Pioneering women actively participate in policy and governance processes to achieve social change. They engage in decision-making bodies, advocate for inclusive policies, and provide their knowledge to design laws, rules, and initiatives that address socioeconomic and gender inequities.

8. Community Development and Grassroots Activism: Pioneering women make a difference at the community level via grassroots activism and community development projects. They work directly with local communities, empowering underprivileged groups, solving social needs, and supporting sustainable development from the bottom up.

9. Research and thinking Leadership: Pioneering women contribute to social transformation via research, thought leadership, and information dissemination. They produce new ideas, question traditional knowledge, and contribute to the creation of evidence-based solutions and policies that address significant social concerns.

10. Cultural and Artistic Expression: Pioneering women in the arts, culture, and media sectors utilize their artistic expressions to question established conventions, promote inclusion, and amplify underrepresented voices. Through their efforts, they increase awareness, create conversation, and inspire social change.

Pioneering women contribute to social change through their acts, ideas, and influence. Their activities pave the path for a more inclusive, fair, and just society, altering institutions, confronting prejudices, and generating possibilities for future generations. By supporting gender equality, social justice, and sustainable development, pioneering women create a lasting effect on society and encourage others to join them in making a difference.

B. Philanthropy, social entrepreneurship, and activism

Philanthropy, social entrepreneurship, and activism are three interwoven techniques that people and organizations utilize to produce positive social effects. Each of these techniques has distinct traits and tactics, but they all have the same purpose of achieving societal change. Here's an explanation of each:

1. Philanthropy: Philanthropy is the act of providing resources, such as financial donations, time, skills, or other types of support, to solve social concerns and enhance the well-being of others. Key elements of philanthropy include:

a. Financial help: Philanthropists provide monies to help non-profit organizations, initiatives, or projects focusing on social problems. This may include gifts to charity foundations, grants to community groups, or direct financial support for people in need.

b. Strategic Giving: Philanthropy frequently includes strategic decision-making to optimize the effect of charitable contributions. Philanthropists may undertake research, analyze needs, and choose beneficial organizations or initiatives to assist. They may also engage with other philanthropists, non-profits, or specialists to leverage resources and create systemic change.

c. Donor Engagement: Philanthropists actively interact with the causes they support. They may engage in fundraising events, offer their time and talents, serve on charity boards, or push for legislative changes that correspond with their philanthropic aims.

2. Social Entrepreneurship: Social entrepreneurship combines entrepreneurial concepts with a focus on tackling social or environmental challenges. Social entrepreneurs establish sustainable company concepts that offer great social impact and financial profits. Key elements of social entrepreneurship include:

a. Innovation and Impact: Social entrepreneurs develop new solutions to social concerns, utilizing business models and market forces to promote sustainable change. They attempt to produce scalable and reproducible solutions that target systemic challenges and enhance the well-being of communities.

b. Sustainability: Social entrepreneurs build company strategies that produce cash while solving social problems. They pursue financial sustainability to maintain long-term viability, enabling them to continue having a positive effect.

c. Systems Thinking: Social entrepreneurs investigate and comprehend the core causes of social issues, including the links between economic, social, and environmental aspects. They attempt to provide comprehensive solutions that address fundamental problems rather than only addressing symptoms.

d. Measurement of Social Impact: Social entrepreneurs analyze and quantify the social impact of their projects, utilizing metrics and indicators to assess their efficacy and make data-driven choices.

3. Activism: Activism entails taking action to bring about social or political change. Activists campaign for particular causes, create awareness, organize communities, and apply pressure on institutions to solve social challenges. Key elements of activism include:

a. Advocacy and Awareness: Activists increase awareness about social concerns, promote certain causes, and campaign for legislative changes or adjustments in public views. They employ numerous venues and strategies to educate the public and shape public dialogue.

b. Grassroots Organizing: Activism frequently includes grassroots organizing, which involves mobilizing people or communities to jointly work towards a common objective. This may involve rallies, marches, community meetings, or internet campaigns.

c. Collaboration and Coalition-Building: Activists engage with like-minded people, groups, or movements to increase their effect.

By creating coalitions, activists combine their efforts, knowledge, and resources to promote larger-scale change.

d. Impacting Institutions: Activists target institutions, including governments, companies, and other prominent organizations, to demand accountability and changes in policies, practices, or attitudes.

Philanthropy, social entrepreneurship, and activism are effective techniques that operate in combination to promote good social change. While philanthropy provides financial resources, social entrepreneurship offers sustainable business models, and activism promotes grassroots movements and structural reforms. Together, these techniques help tackle societal concerns, foster social justice, and build a more equal and inclusive society.

C. Inspiring examples of women using their success for the greater good

There are countless inspirational instances of women who have utilized their prosperity and influence to have a positive effect on society. Here are a few famous examples:

1. Malala Yousafzai: Malala is a Pakistani activist and Nobel laureate noted for her promotion of girls' education. Despite enduring threats and violence, she continues to fight for equitable educational opportunities for girls internationally via the Malala Fund.

2. Oprah Winfrey: Oprah is a media tycoon, philanthropist, and campaigner for several social problems. She has created the Oprah Winfrey Leadership Academy for Girls in South Africa, offering outstanding education and opportunity for impoverished girls.

3. Melinda Gates: Melinda Gates is a philanthropist and co-founder of the Bill & Melinda Gates Foundation. Through her work, she targets topics such as global health, poverty reduction, and gender equality, empowering women and girls globally.

4. Michelle Obama: Former First Lady Michelle Obama is an advocate for education, nutrition, and empowering women. She founded the Let Girls Learn program, which seeks to give education opportunities to millions of girls throughout the globe.

5. Angelique Kidjo: Angelique Kidjo is a Grammy-winning singer-songwriter and UNICEF Goodwill Ambassador. She utilizes her position to campaign for children's rights, education, and women's empowerment in Africa.

6. Serena Williams: Tennis champion Serena Williams actively promotes gender equality, fighting for equal pay and opportunity for women in sports. She also launched the Serena Williams Fund, which focuses on education and empowerment.

7. Wangari Maathai: The late Wangari Maathai was a Kenyan environmentalist and the first African woman to receive the Nobel Peace Prize. She started the Green Belt Movement, which promotes environmental protection, women's rights, and community development.

8. Sheryl Sandberg: Sheryl Sandberg is the Chief Operating Officer of Facebook and the creator of the Lean In Foundation. Through her book "Lean In" and associated efforts, she pushes women to realize their full potential in the workplace and seek leadership positions.

9. Leymah Gbowee: Leymah Gbowee is a Liberian peace campaigner and Nobel laureate. She played a major role in ending the Liberian civil war and encouraging women's engagement in peacebuilding via grassroots organizations and peaceful demonstrations.

10. Amal Clooney: Amal Clooney is a human rights lawyer who defends underprivileged people and organizations globally. She campaigns for justice, freedom of expression, and human rights, notably in instances affecting women's rights and refugee difficulties.

These women serve as encouraging examples of harnessing their success, influence, and resources to create good change. Through their advocacy, charity, activism, and leadership, they have had a substantial influence on problems such as education, gender equality, human rights, environmental protection, and social justice. Their work inspires others and illustrates the transformational potential of harnessing success for the greater good.

CONCLUSION

Redefining Success, Shattering the Glass Ceiling

In conclusion, the road towards redefining success and shattering the glass ceiling is a continual and transforming process. It entails questioning established conventions, pushing for gender equality, and establishing inclusive spaces where women may flourish. By embracing work-life integration, valuing well-being, and advocating diversity and inclusion, we can build a corporate culture that recognizes the talents and possibilities of women.

We must recognize the presence of the glass cliff and negotiate the problems it brings to leadership posts. By applying techniques for overcoming challenges, building support networks, and promoting inclusive environments, we can help women flourish in their professions and attain leadership roles.

Promoting gender equality involves the adoption of policies and programs that address structural prejudices and promote fairness and equal opportunity. By supporting change, building gender-inclusive workplaces, and encouraging diversity and inclusion at all levels of business, we can create conditions where women can flourish and contribute their unique views and abilities.

Empowering future female leaders entails fostering leadership abilities in young girls and women. Through educational efforts, mentoring programs, and access to resources, we can inspire and empower them with the skills they need to become confident and impactful leaders.

Encouraging entrepreneurship and creativity among women is vital for promoting economic development and social transformation. By offering assistance, tools, and networks, we can build an ecosystem that encourages women to achieve their entrepreneurial aspirations and have a lasting effect on society.

Beyond business, pioneering women are having a societal effect. By participating in charity, social entrepreneurship, and activism, they are tackling societal concerns, promoting social justice, and building a more equal society. Their devotion and commitment motivate others to utilize their success for the greater good.

As we continue to redefine success and smash the glass barrier, it is crucial to honor the accomplishments of pioneering women and acknowledge the progress accomplished while noting the work that remains. By promoting an open and supportive corporate environment, we can create a future where women's potential is fully realized and where success knows no borders.

Key takeaways from the book

Key lessons from this book, "Breaking the Glass Ceiling: Pioneering Women Redefining Success in the Business World," include:

1. Redefining Success: This book highlights the necessity of redefining success in the corporate world beyond established metrics and conventions. It invites readers to adopt a larger and more comprehensive definition of success that covers work-life integration, well-being, and personal satisfaction.

2. Shattering the Glass Ceiling: This book explores the hurdles and problems women experience in obtaining leadership roles and breaking through the glass ceiling. It addresses techniques for overcoming these impediments and addressing the special problems that women confront in their professional lives.

3. Work-Life Integration and Well-Being: This book highlights the necessity of work-life integration and emphasizes personal well-being. It urges readers to create a balance that enables them to thrive in their occupations while preserving their physical and emotional well-being.

4. Championing Diversity and Inclusion: This book pushes for diversity and inclusion as indicators of success in the corporate sector. It discusses the advantages of varied viewpoints and experiences and gives ideas on developing inclusive cultures that assist women's growth.

5. Developing Support Networks: This book highlights the necessity of developing support networks for women in leadership roles. It analyzes the importance of mentoring, sponsorship, and networks in giving direction, opportunity, and support for women to achieve.

6. Promoting Gender Equality: This book highlights the necessity of developing policies and activities that promote gender equality in the workplace. It underlines the significance of fighting systemic prejudices and fostering conditions where women have equal opportunity to flourish and prosper.

7. Empowering Future Women Leaders: This book stresses the need to cultivate leadership qualities in young girls and women. It analyzes educational efforts, mentoring programs, and the role of role models in motivating and empowering the next generation of women leaders.

8. Encouraging Entrepreneurship and Innovation: This book underlines the benefits of entrepreneurship and innovation among women. It analyzes approaches to inspire and assist women in following their entrepreneurial dreams and achieving good social change via their companies.

9. Making a Social Effect: This book highlights the capacity of pioneering women to create a social effect beyond their professional achievements. It analyzes the role of philanthropy, social entrepreneurship, and activism in advancing societal change and solving critical concerns.

10. The Path Continues: This book emphasizes that the path to smashing the glass barrier and establishing gender-inclusive workplaces is a continuous effort. It underlines the necessity for continual activism, teamwork, and tenacity to achieve a more equal and inclusive corporate environment.

These key takeaways give readers ideas and assistance on redefining success, overcoming barriers, and contributing to a more inclusive and empowered corporate environment for women.

Inspiring a new era of empowered women in business

In conclusion, inspiring a new era of empowered women in business is a powerful and revolutionary purpose. It needs a joint effort to question current conventions, tear down barriers, and create an inclusive and supportive atmosphere where women may flourish. By adjusting attitudes, supporting leadership development, establishing supportive networks, and fighting for legislative changes, we may provide chances for women to aspire to leadership roles and offer their unique skills and views.

Amplifying success stories, developing inclusive environments, and acknowledging intersectionality are critical components of this path. Collaboration and collaboration across sectors, as well as leading by example, play key roles in inspiring change and empowering women in the corporate world.

By accepting these values and taking action, we can build a new age where women are appreciated, respected, and have equal opportunity to thrive in business. This not only helps women personally but also leads to more diverse, creative, and resilient businesses and society as a whole.

Together, let us continue to inspire and empower women, crafting a future where their voices are heard, their skills are appreciated, and they are important drivers of good change in the corporate world and beyond.

Envisioning a future of gender equality and limitless possibilities

As we envision a future of gender equality and infinite possibilities, we must acknowledge that empowering women in all parts of life, including business, is important for fulfilling this goal. Breaking down barriers, confronting prejudices, and promoting inclusive settings are critical steps towards building a society where women may flourish and contribute to their maximum potential.

By redefining success, cracking the glass barrier, and encouraging a new age of powerful women in business, we can reshape the landscape of opportunity for women. Through mentoring, support networks, and leadership development projects, we can cultivate the abilities and confidence of young girls and women, encouraging them to become the leaders of the future.

It is vital to lobby for legislative reforms that promote gender equality, equitable compensation, and work-life integration. By establishing cultures of respect, diversity, and inclusion, we create places where everyone's skills are acknowledged and celebrated, regardless of gender.

Envisioning a future of gender equality requires identifying and tackling the multidimensional

185

problems that women confront, accepting that development must be inclusive, and respecting the distinctive experiences of women from various backgrounds.

Ultimately, establishing gender equality is a social obligation that involves the engagement and dedication of people, organizations, and society as a whole. By working together, we can build a future where gender doesn't restrict one's capabilities, where women have equal access to opportunities, and where the full potential of all people can be fulfilled.

Let us continue to work towards a future where gender equality is the norm and the boundless potential of every human, regardless of their gender, is released. Together, we can construct a world that is fair, inclusive, and filled with boundless opportunities for everyone.